Dawn Run

Dawn Run

*The Story of a Champion Racehorse
and Her Remarkable Owner*

ANNE HOLLAND

ARTHUR BARKER LIMITED
A Subsidiary of Weidenfeld (Publishers) Limited

Published in Great Britain by
Arthur Barker Limited
91 Clapham High Street
London SW4 7TA

ISBN 0 213 16931 2

Printed in Great Britain by
Butler & Tanner Ltd
Frome and London

Contents

Sadly one character integral to the Dawn Run story is now missing. Dr Eddie Hill, who appeared in robust health and full of *joie de vivre*, suffered a stroke as Charmian was cooking breakfast one morning in February 1985, and died six weeks later without regaining consciousness. With Mrs Hill's permission, I respectfully dedicate this book to his memory.

A. H.

Illustrations

Foreword by Mrs Charmian Hill

When, on a cold winter day in 1971, an English buyer came over to Ireland to try out a young point-to-pointer, no one could have guessed that fourteen years later she would have written a book about that same owner's triple champion-hurdle winner. The point-to-pointer was not sold, but a day's hunting over rough Waterford country ended that first meeting on a happy note.

Anne has produced a very readable account of the swift rise to stardom of Dawn Run, a mare who turned out to have more character than any of us could have foreseen. The hard work that goes into collecting facts, assessing the background and interviewing the various characters connected with what is, after all, only one of hundreds of talented four-legged animals, is shown on the following pages.

The only pity is that the heroine of the story is unable to read it herself.

Acknowledgements

Thanks go first and foremost to Mrs Charmian Hill and the late Dr Eddie Hill for their unfailing help, co-operation, enthusiasm and humour, and to their family.

I am indebted also to Paddy and Maureen Mullins and family; Jonjo O'Neill; John Riordan; Mrs Louisa Mangan; Mr J. J. Harding; Ted Walsh; M. Alan du Breil (Société des Steeplechases de France); Michael Keogh (Irish Turf Club); the Coolmore Stud; Ballsbridge Tattersalls Sales; Edward Gillespie (manager, Cheltenham Racecourse); Peter Smiles (Director Racecourse Security Services); and Sue Montgomery of the *Sporting Life*.

I should also like to thank Stewart Hastie, MRCVS, Grania Wills (*Irish Field*), Jim Old, Mercy Rimell, Jenny Pitman, the Injured Jockeys Fund, the Cotswold Grange, Dean Close School, Navan Racecourse, Maura Toler-Aylward, all the photographers, and to everyone else who has given help and support.

1

The Filly Foal

As twilight fell in rugged Co. Cork, Patrick Mangan looked in on the visiting mare in the foaling box. Her sixth foal was imminent and so he stayed quietly nearby.

Patrick Mangan had always been involved with horses at Curragheen, the family home in Conna, near Mallow, training, racing and breeding them. Among those he bred was the 1956 Champion Hurdle winner, Doorknocker. His seven sons and one daughter followed in his footsteps and one of them, Jimmy 'J.J.', was an amateur rider of some note.

Now the big bay thoroughbred's labours were over. The first thing Paddy Mangan noticed was the pretty white star between the foal's eyes. It was a filly, he saw, and as her coat began to dry he could see it was bay with attractive black points to her legs and the tips of her elegant long ears.

It was 8.30 p.m. on 27 April 1978. Patrick Mangan went into the house to phone John Riordan and tell him that his mare had for a second time produced a healthy filly by Deep Run. The horse was to be named Dawn Run.

The filly foal was soon trying to get her balance and before long was standing on her wobbly legs. She was fast to discover her mother's milk and by the next day she was playful, bucking and kicking around the big, airy stable.

On 29 April, when the foal was two days old, mother and daughter returned to John Riordan's home, Terramount, near Rathcormack. An imposing Georgian country house set back a quarter of a mile from the lane, it was approached by a curving drive through a park-like setting, with a large quadrangled stable-yard behind the house. There the mare and new foal were made comfortable, joined by the cream labrador and terriers scampering about their feet when they were turned out into the iron-railed meadow in front of the house in the mornings.

John Riordan grew up in Rathcormack, a small town on the River Bride where his father Michael ran a grocery shop. His childhood was spent 'always knocking about with horses' and he was secretary of the Avondhu Hunt Club for twelve years. He rode in a few point-to-points, winning on a horse called Littlewood at Fermoy in 1949.

His home, Terramount, was bought by his father in 1930 with one hundred acres for just £2,100, but the family had a tenant in it until John Riordan's marriage to Prudence Kent in 1960, when the young couple moved in.

It is one of several fine Georgian mansions in the area and has high ceilinged, well proportioned rooms and is tastefully decorated. Behind it is the quadrangled stable-yard.

Prudence grew up only four miles away in Castle Lynes and there had always been horses around her family, too. She rode a little, but when they got married they both gave up because of business commitments.

This decision brought about the beginning of the Dawn Run story for John felt he would still like the odd horse around the place; and if he wasn't going to ride, the obvious answer was to have a brood mare.

So he set off to Dublin where at that time the Goffs Sales were still held at Ballsbridge close by the side of the Royal Dublin Horse Show ground. There he met his brother-in-law Jamie Bryan who told him of a yearling filly which he thought might fit the bill.

She was about to be sold and John Riordan never set eyes on her before she entered the ring. He does not profess to be an expert at the breeding game and then in 1961, as now, he was quite happy to heed advice.

So he bid for the little bay yearling filly, Twilight Slave by Arctic Slave out of Early Light, and within moments she had been knocked down to him for three hundred guineas.

There was no need to go and scrutinize his purchase more closely immediately and he went off instead to arrange transport. That achieved, he made his way to Twilight Slave's box – and found it empty! Mildly perturbed and irked more by the inconvenience than anything else, he made his way to the auctioneers to get the matter sorted out.

It transpired that the filly had been taken away by mistake. It was a genuine error, but it was not possible for her to be returned to her rightful owner until the next day. Mr Riordan booked himself some accommodation for the night and took her back to Terramount the next day where she has lived ever since.

When the filly was just two years old he sent her to be covered by Black Tarquin so that, at three and having never been broken let alone allowed to prove herself on the racecourse, she produced a nice big colt foal, a breeder's dream. Sadly, this colt hurt its back as a two year old and had to be put down.

When horses are being bred for National Hunt racing a colt foal is always more welcome than a filly. It will probably be castrated before it is one year old and geldings far outweigh and outnumber mares in terms of racecourse successes and appearances. Statistics show that one third of hurdlers are mares but they represent only one tenth of all steeplechasers.

It is roughly reckoned that it costs about one thousand pounds a year to rear a horse and a National Hunt type is going to be three or four years old before it can be expected to show any return, and then usually only if it is a gelding and has nothing outlandishly wrong with its conformation, or has not befallen some accident meanwhile – and it is horrifying how easily mishaps can happen on even the best fenced and most efficiently run establishments.

Twilight Slave's next foal was another colt, also by Black Tarquin. Named Jaquin, he was sold to a military man in England but never distinguished himself, placing over fences.

Breeding like this was very much merely a hobby, and a loss-making one at that. But thus far Twilight Slave was a good breeder because for the third year running she produced another colt, and this was to be the turning point in her matronly career for this foal was Even Dawn.

A chestnut son of Even Money, Even Dawn won three hurdles including the Aldworth hurdle at Cheltenham, and became one of the best chasers of the mid-seventies, winning eighteen of them, all good class, on premier tracks.

After producing him, Twilight Slave became a less frequent breeder, settling into a pattern of one foal every three years. At the time Menelek was gaining a reputation as a NH sire (he sired Grand National winner Rag Trade later), and Twilight Slave's mating to him produced a chestnut filly Lek Dawn. She was to become the first horse John Riordan kept and put into training, and was ridden by his son Kenty.

Of the Riordans' three children, it is only the eldest Kenty who is interested in horses, and his ambition is to carve a distinguished training career for himself. In the meantime he runs the farm at home. When the Riordans failed to dissuade Kenty from making a career in horses they did the next best thing and sent him to learn the job properly under Padge Berry who trained Lek Dawn for Mr Riordan at his Duncormick, Co. Wexford stables.

Lek Dawn was 'dynamite' as a youngster and when she was being broken in she threw herself to the ground in a terrible temper more than once.

It is often just such a horse, once its aggression is channelled in the right direction, that can prove to be made of the right stuff for racing and with her John Riordan thought he had 'the goods'.

When she won two races and placed several times, it looked as if the sky could be the limit, and ideas of running her at Cheltenham were entertained. But she developed wind trouble and was retired to stud, being the only other mare kept with her mother at Terramount.

Mr Riordan did not like to use the same stallion too often and so after the foaling of Lek Dawn he discussed the next prospective mating with his vet Christy Condon, who suggested that Deep Run, standing at the Sandville Stud, Glanworth, near Fermoy, would be convenient and quite suitable.

The mating produced another filly foal in 1976 to be named Twilight Run, and Mr Riordan sent Twilight Slave back to Deep Run after a barren year, for the mating that was to produce Dawn Run.

The Sandville stud is a part, a very small part, of the vast Coolmore Stud Farms empire. Built up in less than a decade by brothers John and David Magnier, Coolmore has transformed the Irish tradition of casually breeding from the odd mare kept on the farm: it has no fewer than six studs in Ireland, having some of the world's leading sires and also stands stallions in Lexington, Kentucky, in France and in England.

Coolmore, in the heart of Co. Tipperary and only seven miles from the world's master of classic training Vincent O'Brien at Ballydoyle, is the nerve centre of the enterprise, and is run like clockwork.

There is a modern, well equipped laboratory at Coolmore of the highest technical standard for detection and data gathering of every conceivable requirement in the field of equine medicine. Security is provided round the clock by uniformed men with dogs. Among the two hundred and fifty staff are five farriers one of whom, Davy Walsh, has shod six Derby winners, Golden Fleece, Nijinsky, Sir Ivor, The Minstrel, Roberto and Larkspur.

Massive capital injections have led to constant improvements and expansion, including a big new office block at Coolmore where even an artificial lake has been excavated, and a new yard at Thomastown Castle, Co. Tipperary, home of a training centre and yearling 'barns', the American terminology for indoor stables being somehow fitting. They have every modern convenience.

Vincent O'Brien's airstrip is available nearby, and the flat, luxuriant grass-growing plain around Coolmore is ideal for rearing some of the world's best thoroughbreds.

National Hunt racing has for long been the 'poor relation' of the flat industry, with much less money and much more fun involved, and Ireland, traditionally, has always been to the forefront in producing the best of sport and sportsmanship in the winter game, and this is not forgotten by the Magniers, who stand Buckskin, General Ironside and Laurence O at the Beeches Stud, Tallow, and Deep Run at the Sandville Stud.

A narrow, winding road leads to Glanworth from Fermoy until one sees a pair of iron farm gates with a large notice *Sandville Stud – Keep Gates Closed At All Times*.

The stud buildings are not visible from here and without the sign, apparently in the middle of fields dissected by a track, it would be almost impossible to find.

Deep Run is not the most impressive of animals; he does not possess the striking presence of many stallions; he stands only sixteen hands high; his colour, chestnut, is seldom popular; and he is 'over at the knee', a conformation defect which, though it does not cause a horse to break down like being 'back at the knee' does, nevertheless, detracts from his looks.

By Pampered King out of a Court Martial mare, Deep Run won four races, two of them Grade 2, which was enough to list him champion Irish two-year-old in 1968, and was second in the Grade 1 Dewhurst Stakes. At three he was second in the Irish St Leger, and was second to Nijinsky in the Gladness Stakes at four.

He was sold for 6,600 guineas at the Newmarket December Sales and won a two-mile novice hurdle at Doncaster on his jumping debut but ran only twice more before being retired to stud in 1971 at five years old.

So he did not have a startling racing career himself, but as a stallion he certainly has, covering a phenomenal number of mares. He topped the list of NH sires from 1980–85 having produced such as Eckbalco and Golden Cygnet (both tragically killed on the racetrack before fulfilling their enormous potential); Daring Run who won the Irish Champion hurdle; Fifty Dollars More, trained by that gentleman of racing Fred Winter to win the Mackeson Gold Cup at Cheltenham; Another Breeze, Good Crack, Half Free, Deep Gale, Kas, and Dawn Run in a prolific career.

Eckbalco and Daring Run were both placed third in the Champion Hurdle, and Eckbalco also won the Mecca hurdle, the William Hill Imperial Cup on the flat, the Fighting Fifth hurdle, Tia Maria Bula handicap hurdle and the Ladbroke's Christmas Hurdle.

Golden Cygnet had set up a sequence of impressive wins, including the Waterford Crystal supreme novice hurdle at Cheltenham, before being killed in the Scottish Champion Hurdle when disputing the lead at the last flight with the winner and co-favourite Sea Pigeon when six years old.

But none of these names was known in the mid seventies when John Riordan was looking for a likely local stallion for his mare. It is the lot of NH sires that by the time their progeny do any good on the racecourse they are old gentlemen. It also means that the owners of mares who use them in their early years take a distinct gamble as to whether or not they will prove any good.

So when Twilight Slave visited him for the second time his fee was a modest two hundred pounds. By the time Deep Run had made his name he was already in his middle teens, but at least his fee could be dramatically increased, it being £2,000 in 1986.

With her by then shy breeding habits, it was decided not to send Twilight Slave back to stud in 1978, and so it was that she foaled down at Paddy Mangan's, returning to Terramount with the filly foal only two days later.

2

She Nearly Died

The new foal looked no different to any of the past ones and John Riordan, for whom breeding was very much a hobby, took no special notice of her. He let the mare and foal out in the field each morning on his way to work and brought them in each evening on his return.

When the foal was about eight weeks old he went to Killarney for a few days golfing, an even greater hobby for him now that he no longer rode. The golf course at Killarney is nearly as famous as the beautiful lakes and he was looking forward to it. It was a nuisance that Twilight Slave was very sore with gravel (or abscess) in her foot but she would be all right in her stable, for sure.

He could not have been more wrong. The stress caused the mare's milk to dry up. The young foal, suddenly finding its source of nourishment gone, began scalding badly.

By the time Mr Riordan returned from Killarney he could see the filly was seriously ill and called the vet.

But matters were going from bad to worse. The weak little foal's temperature soared to the top of the thermometer. She was very sick and weakening visibly. Worse was to come, for then the temperature plummeted almost to the point of no return. The filly shivered. She could no longer stand and death looked imminent.

'I'm afraid she won't survive,' vet Christy Condon told Mr Riordan as he put her on a drip, then left, unable to do anything more.

Over the next few days Prudence Riordan played a vital

role. Every three hours day and night she went out with a mixture of Complan and glucose to try and coax the foal to feed.

It was a heart-aching, painfully slow, patient job. The foal was desperately weak. She turned her little head away, her eyes dull, her buttocks sore from the scalding. Prudence just knelt in the big stable behind the house, praying, hoping, willing the foal to drink.

Slowly, the filly began to take a little of the liquid. Gradually, she picked up and her strength slowly returned. Eventually, after seven days, she was allowed back out in the field. Thereafter, she always used to come up to the gate for a friendly nuzzle if anyone was passing.

To Prudence, who had many sleepless nights, it was only what she would have done for any sick animal. After the foal recovered she breathed a sigh of relief, thankful it had survived, and went about her normal daily chores again.

When the filly was eight months old, it was time for her to be weaned, and filling the role of mentor at this traumatic phase of any youngster's life was Kenty's old pony, Beaujolais. Beaujolais himself had been saved from death by Mrs Riordan. He suffered from an incurable kidney complaint and eventually the vet came out to put him down, but at the last minute Mrs Riordan successfully pleaded with him not to.

The pony now only had one kidney but was ideal for his new task in life, having a calming influence on a distressed foal freshly separated from its mother. In his heyday he had been a smashing pony and was almost unbeatable on drag-hunts. These were cross-country lines of five or six miles and the little bay could be counted on to reach the end first. But when it came to show-jumping competitions, he could equally be counted upon to knock one down disdainfully.

From October John Riordan fed the foal once a day. It was dark by the time he returned from work and she would be standing by the gate waiting to come in.

So the filly who had nearly died at two months old spent the next two years grazing peacefully at Terramount, until it was time for her to be broken and sold, that being Mr Riordan's policy, apart from Lek Dawn.

The job of breaking fell to Mr J.J. 'Jonjo' Harding, a local farmer and horse-breaker who used to ride in point-to-points; to him, the filly was just another horse. He did not detect any trace of brilliance. He had already broken in her elder brothers and sisters and of them all it was the full sister, Twilight Run, which he thought was going to be *the* racehorse.

Jonjo Harding milked a herd of fifty cows on sixty-five acres at Castletownroche; he used to keep a racehorse but wasn't very lucky, so he took to breaking a few horses instead. His seven children were keen members of the Duhallow Pony Club, enjoying hunting and show-jumping on the three ponies shared between them.

If Lek Dawn, Mr Riordan's choice of *the* horse, had been difficult to break, putting it mildly, her half-sister was an angel. The breaking tackle was put on her for a fortnight. She accepted it all calmly, chewing on the breaking bit with its metal flaps which took her mind off other things. When the leather roller was placed on her back for the first time and gently done up, careful not to pinch her tender young skin, she was busy playing with the bit and barely noticed it.

Mr Harding only had a small stable which meant he had all the more reason to take time and care over his charge, and he did a splendid, patient job.

Once the filly had become accustomed to the tackle, long reins were attached and the lesson of driving began. This meant she had to get used to the reins touching her sides, giving her the aids to move forward or, if there was more pressure on one side or the other to turn the other way so that once she felt the same pressures from a rider's legs she would know what was expected of her. The filly was so quiet, unexpectedly so after the antics of her half-sister Lek Dawn, that Jonjo Harding was soon ready to have her backed.

He held her in the stable, talking to her all the while close to her head, while a lightweight lad patted her on the shoulder. Talking to her all the while, he jumped lightly up and down beside her, his hands on her saddle, then sprang up and lent across her, floppy, like a dummy. She took scant notice of this and so he deftly pulled himself right up into the saddle, easing his weight gently on to her back. She took it all like a lady, and before long he was riding her quietly along the lanes in the company of an experienced older horse.

Now that she was out on the roads it was time for another new experience, that of being shod. Local farrier Michael Walsh came and measured her feet. She had been taught how to pick them up as part of her training and so she obliged now, and before long Michael was banging nails through the insensitive horn, and trimming them just as humans pare their nails.

So, with her basic lessons completed after eight weeks, it was time for her to return home, and John Riordan arrived with his trailer to collect her.

But it was not as simple as that. The youngster would not go into the trailer. Loading is an important lesson in a young horse's life for it fashions the pattern for future years and there is little more irksome than a bad loader. In the older horse it can be caused by sheer bloody-mindedness, but for the youngster it is fear of the unknown. Knowing that this was the case with the filly, John Riordan, Jonjo Harding and his lad were as patient as they could be and tried to cajole her in. It would be fatal to let her 'win', but after blindfolding her, putting a rope around her quarters, and loading another horse to show her the way, they were on the point of giving up. The filly stood rooted to the ground, but in the end she took an almighty leap and plunged in.

Even then the ordeal nearly ended in disaster, for as she did so, legs everywhere, she fell. For an awful moment it looked as if she had broken her leg. Luckily the frightening experience did not leave any permanent detrimental mark on the filly, who was never bad to load again.

Now that she was broken she was entered for the November Ballsbridge Tattersalls Sales and until then Kenty rode her round the farm a bit, popping over some poles, and she proved a natural jumper.

Ballsbridge Tattersalls Ltd was formed and started trading in 1975 as Ballsbridge International Bloodstock Sales. It merged with the Newmarket firm of Tattersalls in 1979, and it holds a number of specialized sales each year.

The principal ones are the Derby Sale, probably the leading NH sale in Ireland or England, held on the eve of the Irish Derby; the September Yearling Sale, the first major yearling sale of the year in Europe; the November NH Sale at which this filly was sold; and the December Flat-bred Sale, held immediately after the Tattersalls December Sale.

Veterinary surgeon Willie O'Rourke is managing director, and the board of directors includes the Tattersalls chairman Michael Watts; Irish National Stud chairman Larry Ryan; and Alan Lillingstone. Mr Lillingstone is Master of the famous Limerick Hunt and was one of the best amateur riders, winning the Champion Hurdle on Winning Fair in 1963; also, as a three-day-event rider, he won a European team gold medal in 1979; and, at his Mount Coote Stud, he bred Deep Run.

Nothing else was done specifically to prepare the filly for the Sales. She was not kept in, or groomed, or fed pounds of oats to make her fat and sleek. She was still very much the gawky, long-legged schoolgirl, growing rapidly and yet to fill out. She looked as if she would need plenty of time.

Nevertheless John Riordan entered her for the pre-Sale Show the day before. He felt she was the best looking, a superb mover with lovely limbs, but was obviously unfurnished, and was well pleased when she finished second in the show for which one of the judges was Ireland's leading NH trainer Paddy Mullins.

The next day Mr Riordan nearly withdrew the filly from the Sales. It is well understood that the best place in an auction is in or near the middle of the day. Late lots can suffer because prospective purchasers have already bought what they want and early lots can be worse still because buyers have either not yet arrived or decide to wait and see if something better comes along later. Understandably, it is horses which either have bad form or poor pedigree or both which are allocated these lots.

Imagine John Riordan's disgust, then, when he found his filly had been put in early, at Lot 29. It was all the more surprising because her full sister Twilight Run had fetched a useful 7,600 guineas from a prime position two years earlier.

He had a good mind to take her home. But the auctioneer was good, and conjured up bids for her well.

Not surprisingly, John Riordan found considerable interest in his filly at the Sales on that November day in 1981, for she moved well, was big and was superbly bred for chasing. Her granddam Early Light (by Cheltenham Gold Cup winner Fortina) won four point-to-points (over banks) and bred two winners; and her great-granddam Broken Dawn won on the flat, over hurdles and fences and bred eight winners, including that crack chaser Brasher, who won the Scottish Grand National and the Grand National trial and was placed in the Whitbread Gold Cup, the Hennessy Gold Cup, and the Tote Champion Novices Chase at the National Hunt Festival at Cheltenham.

But there was one major drawback for this sale. The filly was the 'wrong' sex, and although some improvement and encouragement had been made on behalf of NH mares with the introduction of mares-only races in 1966, there was still considerable market reluctance against them.

It did benefit breeders indirectly, for the progeny of a winner can be expected to fetch more money when sold. Winners, too, are frequently given concessions by way of reduced stud fees. The policy began to make itself felt in comparison with English breeders for prospective buyers flocked increasingly to Ireland where more dams had won on the racecourse than in England by virtue of having a number of races with no male rivals.

Waking up to this aspect, England introduced a series of eight mares-only races sponsored by Hoechst Regumate in 1982 culminating with a valuable final at Newbury.

And for the 1983–4 season, England introduced an across-the-board five pounds weight allowance for all mares in non-handicaps regardless of record, a similar three pounds allowance having begun in Ireland in 1983.

John Riordan met all sorts of people when selling his horses. Prospective purchasers had to find out all they possibly could before committing themselves in the auction ring. They might, after all, be staking several thousand pounds on an animal that they had seen for no more than a few minutes standing in a strange box and trotting up and down the concrete outside. An awful lot has to be taken on trust, and trust can all too often evaporate at such a time.

Inevitably, would-be buyers will pan a horse, commenting on its less good points and will often adopt an 'I know it all' attitude. One such in the case of John Riordan's filly was a woman trainer from England who came to see her.

The catalogue description of the filly was naturally brief, as she had not yet done anything. It stated simply, 'This filly is broken.'

To break or not to break a youngster before a sale can leave the breeder the loser either way: unbroken, and a possible buyer may not have the time or inclination to do the job himself, he wants something to go on with straight away.

Or, if the youngster is broken in, there will be those people who decide that the horse has been 'tried', that is, tested at the gallop and found to be lacking in some way, hence it is up for sale.

The woman trainer adopted this attitude.

'She's obviously been tried,' she stated to the quiet demeanoured Mr Riordan.

'In that case, you obviously know more than I do,' he replied softly and left it at that.

Another English trainer was ecstatic about the filly. She had everything; looks, breeding, temperament; everything, that is, except the 'right' sex.

'I daren't tell you what I'd give for her if she were a gelding,' he told Mr Riordan sincerely.

Another trainer claimed he wanted to buy the filly before she came to the Sale, but that Mr Riordan had asked too much for her. But in fact, he never got as far as asking the price! There was another to whom he did ask a price of eight thousand pounds.

'He could have offered me four thousand pounds, then we could have split the difference at six thousand pounds – there you are, that's very close to the figure she did make!' he says in true Irish dealing fashion.

But there was one person who was convinced the mare, on her breeding alone, would make ten thousand pounds – and that would be out of her reach. Still, she would go the Sales and see. . . .

3

Charmian Hill

That person was Mrs Charmian Hill who had, at the age of sixty-one, come within a hair's-breadth of paralysis.

By all normal standards she should never have ridden again, let alone raced. But by any normal standards, a perfectly healthy woman of that age would not have contemplated racing at all, beyond watching sedately through a pair of binoculars.

All Ireland knew, however, that Mrs Hill was no ordinary woman, and her courage, bravery, dash and skill, and not a little eccentricity, were admired almost on a level that was later to be reserved for her mare.

Charmian Hill is an energetic, spry, intelligent woman for whom motherhood alone, while fulfilling, was not enough. Always alert, her piercing eyes darting about, her quick voice ever enthusiastic be it for or against a given matter, she is always busy doing something, and is remarkably fit. She embarked upon a racing career at an age when most jockeys have already given up, and is still riled that she was forced to quit when she was sixty-three.

Charmian Hill, née Orpen, grew up in different parts of Ireland, but it was the holidays at her grandfather's home, Monksgrange in Co. Wexford, where the River Boro rises and runs down to the Slaney that she loved best.

Her grandfather was the historian G.H. Orpen, and so the day-to-day running of the farm was left to her grandmother.

The young Charmian's early education was in a Dublin rectory but she lived for the holidays when she could get to

Monksgrange. Neither her mother nor her father were in the least bit horsey, nor her elder sister Virginia nor brother John. But the first thing Charmian would do was run out to find the donkey, put on a headcollar and ride it bareback round the farm, sometimes tumbling off, always quickly jumping on again.

She adored the country life and was thrilled when her parents moved into Monksgrange when she was eleven. With the move came her first pony Bungie, so named because he was like an india-rubber ball. He had a mind of his own but it taught the little girl a lot more than a perfect pony which only required sitting on would have.

It was with Bungie that Charmian first tasted the delights of hunting, following the Bree hounds with a zeal that was already marking her as a kid with guts and enterprise. It was to lay the foundation for later years when she would become one of Ireland's best-known lady riders.

Nowhere on earth can rival hunting in Ireland and the south-east corner of Wexford and Waterford has remained largely unchanged by agriculture, wire, tourists, or shooting. Here the country is rugged and wild, presenting a challenge and one of life's great thrills to cross.

The attitude was relaxed and friendly, and the little girl soon found herself hacking many miles to join in the sport. Something stirred in her heart as hounds were put into covert, a clump of gorse atop a rocky outcrop, with a river winding its course peacefully through the valley below.

They were tough, hard hounds, and tough, friendly people who followed them. The ground was rough and stony, a mixture of dry stone walls and banks dividing the rough fields.

Charmian soon learnt to take the banks from a trot, to give her pony his head and to sit tightly in the middle of the saddle as he popped up, and then off, stretching in mid-air to clear the ditch on the landing side.

He had to be nimble and sure-footed, also, to cope with the terrain, the unexpected holes, patches of heather giving way to stony tracks or lumpy. centuries-old turf. The girl had to be sharp and quick-witted, too. She learnt to use her eyes, to go the shortest way so that her pony could keep up, to listen and to watch.

She learnt to slip her reins and lean well back as she dropped steeply down off a wall on to the slippery road below. She learnt which rivers were too big to cross and where the fords were. She thought nothing of a couple of wet feet if wading through a deep bit enabled her to keep up with the pack in full cry. She scrambled up banks and brushed through thorns and nonchalantly jumped the few bits of wire to be found.

Sometimes hounds checked as they swung towards the sea, the waves almost lapping their feet. The view was breathtaking, the excitement of the chase exhilarating and her eyes lit up with the thrill of it all. Often she hacked eight or more miles home.

Then came the difficult bit. Tiredness would set in during the evening, but her non-horsey family did not understand and she *had* to keep her eyes open. If she let her weariness show she would be stopped from her next day's hunting and she could not contemplate that. She *lived* for it.

As a teenager Charmian joined her elder sister Virginia at boarding school in England, Manor House, Limpsfield, Surrey. It was a musical school and the headmistress Miss Everett had been the music teacher of Charmian's mother when she was at school.

Charmian's riding was necessarily limited while there but she met other girls with like interests and her time passed happily enough. There were a hundred girls and one of Charmian's contemporaries was Sir Winston Churchill's daughter Mary, now Lady Soames.

Both the Orpen girls were bright, especially Virginia who was also particularly musical. A brilliant academic career looked in prospect for her when she went up to Oxford to read modern languages at a time when it was still very difficult for girls to get there, but sadly Virginia suffered a brain tumour when she was twenty-one and died.

Charmian, though not particularly musical – she learnt to

play the piano, like everyone then – followed her rural bent by reading agriculture at Trinity, Dublin, only the second girl ever to do so, after spending a while at a 'school for older girls' in Germany, staying with her cousin.

While at Trinity she kept a horse at home and hunted as often as she could, but any thoughts of point-to-pointing then was ruled out of court. She had a horse called Boro Lass who would have been good enough but her parents said it was too dangerous and in those days children respected their parents' wishes.

It was at Trinity that Charmian met the irrepressible Eddie Hill. He was studying to become a doctor and in him she met her match. He sparkled with a *joie de vivre* and was a hard man to keep down, bubbling with enthusiasm from the twinkle in his eyes to the frequent smiles spreading from the corners of his lips. He was a fun-loving student with many girlfriends and lots of high spirits and it was not always easy to tell when he was being serious. His student friends found this too, and were at pains to remind him when he had committed himself to Charmian.

One of the annual hops at Trinity was the zoo dance and it was at that that the young medical student asked Miss Orpen, whom he had met there two years earlier, to marry him. She accepted and amidst much merriment they celebrated until the early hours, finally going home considerably the worse for wear.

Knowing the incorrigible Eddie of old, his friends thought perhaps he might forget the very public commitment he had made the previous night, so they kept ringing him during the day to remind him, 'Don't forget you got engaged last night!'

The couple both received their degrees – a Master of Science for Charmian – when he was twenty-four and she was twenty-one and they were married soon afterwards.

Born in Dublin, Eddie Hill was the fourth of his parents' eight children; his father was a rector and during the early 1900s both his parents were missionaries in Japan.

Many of life's lasting qualities were formed firmly in Eddie's mind during his childhood. He had three elder sisters, then he was the first of three boys in a row, followed by another sister and finally the youngest brother, all to be fed, clothed and educated on a rector's stipend.

The Rev. Louis Hill cut the children's hair and mended their shoes. If they wanted to get anywhere, they went by bike. The rectory was open house and people were always coming in and out. It was a life not dissimilar to the one Eddie finally chose as a doctor, meeting lots of people, most of whom were coming with problems of one sort or another, often marital, that needed sorting out sympathetically.

Money might have been tight but the children thrived on the upbringing. Four of them went to university, Eddie gaining a scholarship to Trinity. He, too, went to school in England, there being few schools in Ireland for the $2\frac{1}{2}$ per cent Protestant population, and at Dean Close, Cheltenham, parsons' sons had a ten per cent reduction in fees. Something that happened there formed a lasting impression on him.

The school was in danger of closing down and the masters worked for a year without pay in order to save it. Obviously they had just enough to live on, but it gave the young Eddie great respect and admiration for them and a determination never to join a union or similar association where such a gesture would surely never be made.

Dean Close was founded by the Rev. (later Dean) Francis Close in 1884 and opened two years later. It is situated in Lansdowne Road, Cheltenham, and it was impossible to foretell the significant part that spa town, and more particularly its racecourse set beneath beautiful Cleeve Hill, would play in Eddie Hill's future. Horses formed no part of his Dublin rectory childhood at all. He probably would not even have realized that horse-racing took place at Cheltenham at all had it not been for the fiery, hard-hitting sermons preached against it at his school. So instead of the sport being an insignificant, neutral pastime of other people, he was brought up positively against it. Indeed, the school's founder is said to have had the boys marching round the course at Prestbury Park, waving banners protesting against its evils.

Dawn Run and Charmian Hill parade for the crowd at Tramore in May 1984, led by Jack Evoy.

Charmian Hill on Johnny beating Lord Waterford at the Curraghmore
Point-to-Point in 1960.

Above and below: Boro Nickel, on whom Mrs Hill won many point-to-points.

New Year's Day 1974 at Fairyhouse: Mrs Charmian Hill was the first woman to ride against men under Irish Rules.

Mrs Hill in the rough and tumble of National Hunt racing. *Above:* on The Jester, and *below* on Yes Man, with whom she was to have a terrible accident.

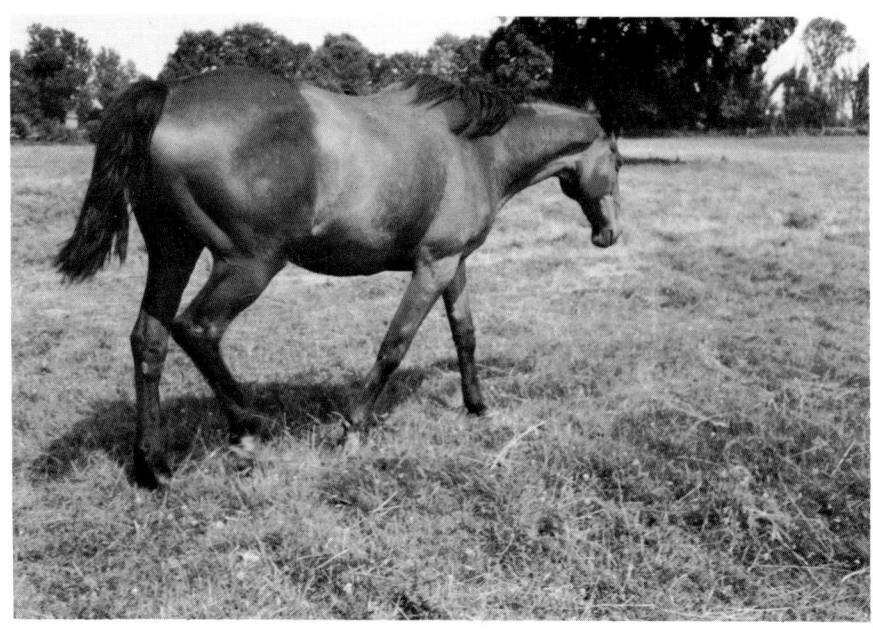

Dawn Run's maternal granddam, Early Light.

Dawn Run's dam, Twilight Slave.

Her sire, Deep Run, and (*below*) her half-sister and niece, where
Dawn Run spent her early life.

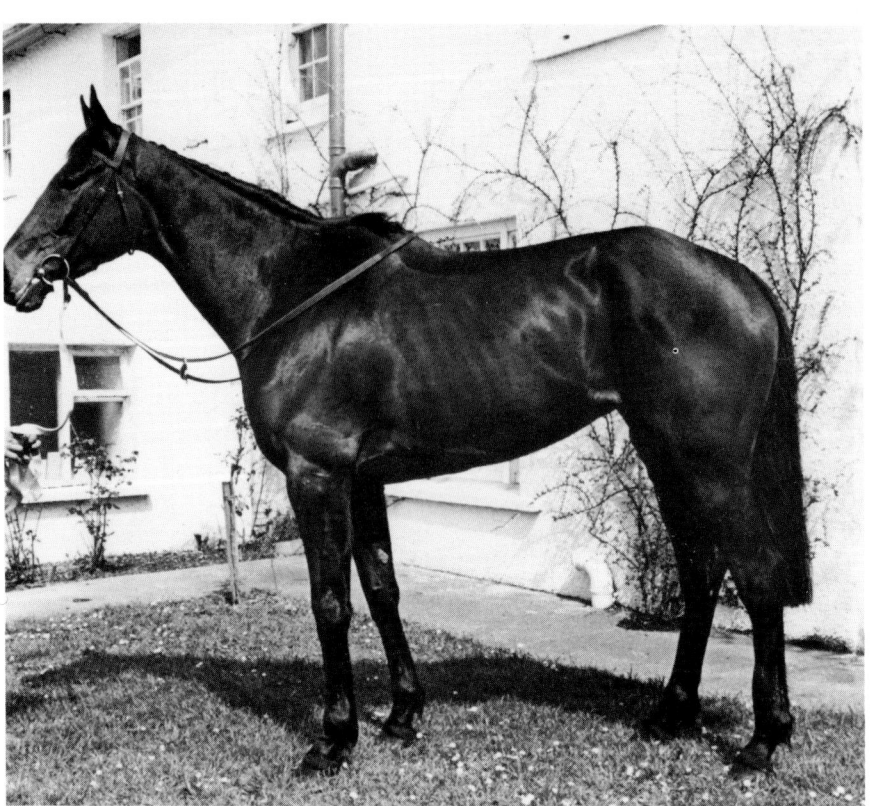

Dawn Run (with pedigree).

			Prince Chevalier
		Pampered King	Netherton Maid
	Deep Run		
		Trial by Fire	Court Martial
			Mitraileuse
Dawn Run			
(1978)			Arctic Star
		Arctic Slave	Roman Galley
	Twilight Slave		
	(1962)		Fortina
		Early Light	Broken Dawn

But boys will be boys and when something is out of bounds, its fruits suddenly seem very tempting. So it was that the demure young gentlemen of Dean Close found their own way of participating in the banned sport.

When Eddie was there, there were among the non-teaching staff Raven, who shone their shoes, and Finch, who stoked the furnace, and between them they managed surreptitiously to take the boys' bets. It was in the heyday of Golden Miller, five times winner of the Cheltenham Gold Cup and of one Grand National. It was just like having money printed for the boys. Every time they wagered sixpence on Golden Miller, they could be virtually sure of getting 1/6d back!

Eddie Hill was seventeen before he ever set foot on a race-course, and then it was with a sense of guilt, feeling his father would have frowned on it. Never could he have guessed how embroiled he was to become in the sport.

In fact when he met Charmian at Trinity he probably did not realize how big a part horses played in her life for she seldom rode while at university. But she dragged him along to a few point-to-points and he enjoyed them so much that soon he seldom missed one.

The first thing Eddie Hill did after qualifying and marrying in 1940 was to join the Irish Army. His pay was £28 per month and that included doctor's allowance and captain's allowance. He was demobbed in 1943 and went to Rotunda Hospital, the world's most famous maternity hospital, where he studied for an extra degree in gynaecology and obstetrics and went on to become a leading figure in that world.

But first he had to set up practice. To do that he simply had to buy a house, put up a plate, and hope for patients, for there was no National Health Service in Ireland. The town he chose was Waterford.

4

Family Life

Eddie and Charmian cycled forty miles from Enniscorthy to search for a suitable home in Waterford. He liked the city because it combined town and country, so his young wife would be able to hunt and he could still enjoy town life.

He pedalled across the Redmond Bridge spanning the River Suir and into the historic grey-slated town centre with its attractive wide streets and fine Georgian buildings. He passed some of the walls and fortifications built round the fifteen acres of city by the Norsemen in the ninth century and cycled along the quayside to where Parnell Street meets the Mall by the imposing circular Reginald's Tower.

Waterford is best known for its crystal glass factory on the southern outskirts of the town where groups of tourists are shown round every ten minutes during the summer and at regular intervals throughout the rest of the year. The blazing furnaces are kept at a constant temperature of 2552 degrees Fahrenheit. The glass blowers and engravers are apprentices for five years and every single piece of glass is hand cut using a single blade and all the engraving is done entirely freehand. Truly the glass is fashioned by craftsmen and sought after the world over.

Waterford Crystal sponsor many sporting occasions, including three hurdle races on the opening day of the Cheltenham National Hunt Festival, the £20,000 Waterford Crystal supreme novices, the £26,000 Waterford Crystal stayers, and the £55,000 Waterford Crystal Champion Hurdle itself.

Eventually Dr Hill found a run-down Georgian house

which he was able to buy for four hundred pounds. It had a huge key, old-fashioned Victorian wallpaper which was peeling off the well-proportioned rooms, and most of the windows were broken. Eddie and Charmian moved into the top storey and set about doing it up.

If the door-bell rang, Eddie would run down to answer it, stripping off his painting overalls on the way, hoping it might be a prospective patient, but all too often it was someone like the butcher's boy delivering.

Charmian soon managed to rent a stable for her hunter and used to cycle two miles each way to tend him. She joined the Waterford Hunt and enjoyed many good days on him. During this time Eddie, ever the extrovert, became increasingly in demand as an entertainer, and toyed with the idea of joining the Magic Circle. He was marvellous with children, transmitting his own *joie de vivre* to his captivated audience at their parties. He entertained adults, too, and sometimes 'sawed' an unsuspecting volunteer in half! But all this lapsed as his practice built up and his reputation grew. Never a man to shirk a challenge, he became a pioneer and was the first doctor in Ireland to induce labour using a drip.

The local nuns were horrified; they thought it dreadfully sinful to interfere with nature and they prayed in chapel because they thought it couldn't possibly be right for childbirth to be so painless. And they were afraid something terrible would happen like rupturing the uterus.

Two years after he had begun this method Eddie was amused to read an article advocating the induction of labour for the way it speeded things up. But the writer claimed it should only be done in hospital and not for first babies, whereas Eddie used it in patients' homes and *especially* for first babies.

Not long after they were married Eddie and Charmian acquired what was to become a lifelong love of travelling, when they answered an advertisement in the *British Medical Journal* for an exchange with a Danish doctor. After that they were to visit China, Hong Kong, Australia, America and the Himalayas.

Their visit to the Himalayas was made, in impulsive Hill

style, 'on spec'. The first thing they did on arrival was to hire a houseboat. By chatting to the man leasing it, they found he could arrange a trip into the mountains, for several days' climbing.

He arranged absolutely everything for them, from guides to food and equipment to so many servants that they did not even have to carry their own handkerchiefs.

Their love of travelling was often difficult to pursue in the early days because of Eddie's work. A baby might be imminent, so they would stay home two weekends in a row waiting for it, then decide to go away the next weekend when of course it would decide to arrive.

But it was rewarding, absorbing work. 'People who don't have children don't know what they are missing,' he declared. The Hills' life was enriched by four, Jeremy, Oliver, Penny and, after a considerable gap, Barton.

It was not long before Mrs Hill had them all on ponies but none of them took to her passionate love for hunting. Although Oliver was potentially the best he, like the others, took to alternative sports, in his case ski-ing, and he and Penny both enjoyed marathon running.

The three boys attended Dean Close and Penny was educated at a Quaker convent in Waterford.

As they were growing up, Eddie decided it might be time to call it a day with gynaecology and opt for a branch of the profession offering more predictable hours, so he closed down his practice and went to study rheumatology in St Thomas' Hospital, London, for four months.

It was a gamble, and when he returned to Waterford he had lost all his patients; but within a week he had redoubled them, and became doctor for a school, a factory, two convents, the electricity board and other institutions, as well as to many private patients.

It was not a practice to make the couple millionaires; two-thirds of his income went on expenses, like a secretary and a car, and competition was fierce, but it was a way of life he loved and they were well enough off to consider moving to a house with some land.

Eddie for many years coveted a property called Belmont at Ballinakill on the outskirts of Waterford, and with admirable timing, as his practice flourished and his children were nearly through school, it came on the market and they bought it for £8,500 with thirty-three and a third acres.

Its situation was idyllic. To reach it, they turned off the Waterford to Dunmore road, just past the Ardkeen Hospital, down a nearly hidden lane which led to the River Suir. Just before its banks, they turned left over a cattle grid into the area of permanent pasture, dotted by beech trees. The drive carved its way through the middle until, crossing another cattle grid by a walnut tree, it swept round in front of the unpretentious, colonial-style house. It was neither parti-cularly imposing nor majestic but the view certainly was.

The park-like land sweeps down to the river which stretches round to the right where it is split by an island with a castellated folly on it. The river here is tidal and the shipping channel runs along the far bank.

The creeper-covered house is mostly on one floor, and is approached by a short flight of steps to a blue door. The previous owners had pulled down all but the basement in the 1930s and rebuilt the present house which the Hills have left unchanged. Inside it was cool and pleasant and Charmian soon stamped her own mark on it, making it comfortable without being luxurious, what one might term 'lived in'.

The two old, red and white painted stables at the back in a stone yard were in such a good state of repair that Char-mian never had to replace so much as a tile (the sort of job she would have done herself) and it was not long before she had her hunter, Johnny, installed.

Beyond the yard was three-quarters of an acre of walled garden. One of the first things Eddie did was to have a swimming pool built, laying the flagstones himself, and they used it constantly, often both of them starting and ending the day with a quick dip. He laid out the garden around it with shrubs and plants which are now mature and add a splendid touch of colour and design. There is a tall palm, which in summer has dozens of white flowers cascading like fireworks from it.

37

A mill wheel, a small statue and old flower-filled stone troughs all add to the character.

Pears grow on the high wall by the lawn, bounded by a hedge with an archway leading into the biggest part of the garden reserved for growing vegetables. This soon became a strictly segregated domain: Mrs Hill tended the fruit, Dr Hill the vegetables, but both, with great rivalry, grew potatoes.

It was the start of days full of fun, a word which was used with happy regularity in the Hill household, spiced with many lively conversations and spirited arguments inevitable between two such intelligent and strong characters.

Eddie never allowed himself or their home to become dominated by his wife's love of horses: his love of contemporary art, for instance, found his choice of paintings vying more successfully for wall space than hers of horses, which were confined to the sunny little study.

Summer breakfasts, after a quick swim, were idyllic, and ones that did not include fresh fruit, strawberries, raspberries, loganberries, rhubarb or blackcurrants, were rare. When it was just the two of them breakfast was in the unmodernized quarry-tiled kitchen, kept warm by an Aga, where a big Welsh dresser took up most of one wall. When the family was home they ate in the dining-room which contained large, polished furniture and a sideboard groaning under the food.

Mrs Hill seldom had help in the house and was always busy doing at least two jobs at once. No wonder she remained as light as a feather, for she was always on the go and was inclined to spend far more time with her hunter than in the house.

It was a congenial, relaxed family home enjoying the best climate of anywhere in Ireland with as much sun as Valentia but less rain, and to which the Hill children, as they grew up, amiably repaired.

Jeremy, the eldest, became a senior pilot with Aer Lingus, married an Australian girl, and later provided the Hills with their first grandchildren, two boys and a girl. In 1984 they went to Australia for two years to taste life there. In the summer of 1984 Jeremy inherited Monksgrange from his uncle, Mrs Hill's brother John, and so the Co. Wexford home where Mrs Hill spent the happiest days of her childhood and learnt to ride, will echo to the sounds of family life once more.

The Hills' daughter Penny was the only one to follow into the medical profession, becoming a physiotherapist and in 1984 she was undertaking a three-year course in acupuncture, the 'pin pricking' alternative medicine which is gradually becoming recognized.

Oliver, a bearded, bright-eyed, easy-going young man, set up in business in Dublin, running a building development company and a dry-cleaners. This left him with firm views on the reasons for Ireland's economic problems, believing that the harder someone worked the more he was taxed with no incentive to employ people.

Barton went through a long-haired hippy stage after he left school before settling down in London as an antique furniture restorer.

All four married and produced a total of nine grandchildren for the Hills, but only Jeremy's marriage remained intact. With divorce not allowed in Ireland, the other three separated.

5

The Galloping Granny

Once the children were teenagers and away at school, Charmian found time on her hands and turned her attentions more to horses, and for the first time, racing. It all began in 1959 when, at the age of forty, she rode Johnny in the local hunt members' race. Wearing hunting dress, she finished second to Lord Waterford.

She reversed the placings the following year to sample on her second race ride that special feeling of riding a winner and so she determined to buy herself a real point-to-pointer.

She spotted a horse called Sadlers Clerk winning a race at Wexford and managed to buy him for eight hundred pounds. She hunted him and prepared him for racing as best she knew how, then took him to a cousin of Eddie's at Tallow who had offered a stable and groom to help get him ready for the day's race.

The groom, it transpired, knew as little about racing as Mrs Hill. She simply picked it up as she went along, sometimes the hard way, as was the case when the saddle slipped on Sadlers Clerk, depositing her on the ground just as she was challenging at the second last fence. She had never heard of a surcingle. ...

Charmian Hill loved those point-to-pointing days. It was hard work when she had two to take, saddle up, ride, and then bring home again. Jim Evoy, the helper, did not drive and one day she cracked some ribs when her horse slipped up on the flat. After that Jim's brother Jack used to go with her to drive. It was very much her own thing that she was enjoying. Very occasionally she would send a horse that was too difficult for her to Willie O'Grady to be trained, giving her the odd runner under Rules, but really it was having one or two at home, which she could ride herself, that she liked best.

In 1970 Sunday point-to-pointing was introduced in Ireland, with betting permissible, but no bar, so spectators brought their own drink, and this brought the crowds rolling in. With the start of Sunday racing, the local shop-keepers would ask Mrs Hill where the next meeting was, and go and cheer her on.

The price of land had roughly quadrupled since the sixties and this brought a problem of where to stage point-to-points because with their land suddenly being so valuable, owners became reluctant to have several dozen horses and several hundred cars churn it up. It resulted in many courses being built on the inside of NH courses, but with nothing like the same atmosphere.

A problem a lightweight like Mrs Hill found was the dearth of ladies' races in Irish point-to-points. Ladies' races are a feature of the English scene and source of much light-hearted, chauvinistic banter: they go so fast because they can't control their horses, and so on. In reality, at eleven stone, they carry a stone or a stone-and-a-half less than the men's races, and this became Mrs Hill's biggest bone of contention in racing. (Since 1976 in England all but men's open races have been open to women riders as well.) She felt it put women riders at a disadvantage and made owners reluctant to put them up.

She was adamant that all lady riders should have a weight allowance (as, indeed, mares now have!) and she campaigned for it unsuccessfully for years.

Weighing only eight stone herself, Mrs Hill's horses always had to hump at least four stones, and sometimes five, of crushing dead weight on their backs to compete on level terms against the men.

Inevitably it meant that there were far fewer lady riders in Ireland, which can only detract from the sport. There are many fine and fearless horsewomen who would be greatly

41

admired point-to-pointing. In the next few years Mrs Hill rode a total of eighteen point-to-point winners, seven of them on the tiny Boro Nickel.

Bought as a hunter because she looked too small to race, the bay mare stood just 15.1½hh in her shoes, and there are not many of that size who would not only carry, but win, under 12st 10lb!

Mrs Hill hunted her for two years, and discovered when galloping across fields during a good hunt one day that the mare had a good deal of speed. As she was without a point-to-pointer at the time, she decided to try the little mare, with great success. Boro Nickel was so small that when conditions were terribly wet or windy, Charmian tucked her in behind other horses to get shelter!

The gutsy little mare won or was placed nearly every time she ran until she was eleven years old, when she won what transpired to be her last race. It was on firm ground and the mare finished with a bit of a leg so Mrs Hill decided to breed from her. She became Mrs Hill's foundation brood mare, and now roams the acres of Belmont with her offspring, joined in the summer by the hunter and current point-to-pointer.

Not all that long after she took up point-to-pointing, Mrs Hill became a grandmother; someone from the press discovered this and christened her the Galloping Granny which she has been dubbed ever since, but she didn't mind at all. She has become quite used to her age being a topic of conversation.

Some of the papers' headlines were 'Galloping Granny Going Strong'; 'Not Me, Says the Racing Granny'; and 'Galloping Grannie Still Wants to be a Jockey'. Racegoers often called out to her, too.

There was a time when Dr Hill overheard two spectators discussing race prospects. Mrs Hill was changing in the horsebox – there being no facilities at Irish point-to-points for women – and he heard one say to the other, 'Look at the old woman who's going to ride in a race, I wouldn't be backing her.'

'You wait and see,' Dr Hill interjected; and she won.

There was another time when a group of disgruntled race-goers who had obviously lost money on her, called out as she rode in, ''Ere, 'ol lady, what do you think you're doing? You shouldn't be racing!'

And once at Ballynoe, a little point-to-point course on the side of a hill about thirty miles from Waterford, as Mrs Hill and Jack Evoy arrived, squeezing the box in through the narrow gateway, large, wet snowflakes began to fall. It was, in her words, 'one of those side slipping courses with no level ground and no straight run'. Mrs Hill hated those small circuits 'where you go round three times over the same ground like a whirlygig'.

Walking the course as the snow flurried down it was as she feared: left-handed, on the same leg the whole way, with a sharp downhill run and a long climb up again to a very short straight to the winning post after the last fence. The fences were stiff but well made.

The snow stopped but had made the ground soft and slippery as Mrs Hill struggled back from the weighing tent to the horsebox carrying her two-stone saddle and stone of lead, to saddle up Ilando. He was a strong puller which she raced in a bit with two rings (called a scorrier or Cornish snaffle) to give her more control. Ilando had already won two point-to-points that season and was favourite now, but there was a fast horse in the race which might use its speed to advantage on the little circuit. As usual, Mrs Hill was the only lady rider. And also as usual, she was much the oldest.

The tension always mounts before a race no matter how many times you have ridden, especially when you are on a fancied horse, and Mrs Hill was no exception. Will your horse get a clear view of the first fence? Will another horse gallop across you or fall in front of you? Will he act on the ground? Once mounted, the butterflies leave the stomach, and as the first few fences flick safely by the adrenalin starts to flow.

The crowd perched on top of the hill began to mutter as the favourite was last of the remaining five runners as they set out on the last short circuit. Ilando was hating the slush and Mrs Hill had not hustled him. Now it was time to give

43

him the message to go; shortening the reins, she gave him a kick and a sharp backhander.

'Now, boy, get going.'

He responded by lowering his head and lengthening his stride, and he quickly passed two horses. But the two leaders were a long way clear. To the hilltop spectators it looked a hopeless task.

Then Ilando made one of his rare blunders at the second last, pecked badly, and all indeed looked lost.

But Mrs Hill does not give up easily, a quality she transmits to her horses.

'Stop acting like a mule,' she yelled at him as she chucked him up and drove with all her force to the last fence.

Ilando's response to the reprimand was electrifying. He passed the second horse but as they reached the last fence the leader was still six lengths clear. Ilando simply flew, racing into the last as if it was not there, hurdling it at breakneck speed, and the pair set about catching the leader.

Halfway up that short run-in, they reached the leader's quarters. In another two seconds they were past and scored by an amazing two lengths. It was the sort of thrill that makes all the effort, all the heartbreaks, all the bruises and broken bones worthwhile. The roar from the appreciative crowd rose in a crescendo from the hilltop.

It was a sound that split the clouds better than any sun and as they rode into the enclosure poor Ilando suffered pats and slaps on the rump which under other conditions would have seen him let fly with his heels.

Everyone wanted to congratulate her and as she walked back to her car an elderly countryman stretched out his hand to pump hers and said, 'Now, m'am, do you not t'ink it is time you retired? Sure, you are as old as meself and 'tis not fitting to be riding at our age!'

6

Charmian Makes History

In the early seventies, Mrs Hill was excited to learn that the Irish National Hunt Steeplechase Committee would allow women to apply for licences to ride in amateur NH races.

When Mrs Hill's previous trainer Willie O'Grady died, she wanted to find one that was not too far away. Never a Sunday-morning-phone-call-owner, it was always her intention to keep fully involved with her horses. To proffer a sugar lump was not enough, she wanted to ride herself and, thirty-six miles away from her Waterford home, Paddy Mullins at Gorsebridge was just close enough. In those days it was comparatively easy to get into Paddy's stable. Now he is described by some as a more brilliant trainer than Vincent O'Brien.

Sundancer was the first horse she put with him and this was the horse on which, at the age of fifty-six, she became the first woman to take advantage of the new rule. It made headline news in Ireland and even a front page paragraph in an Australian daily paper.

It seems incredible now, only just over a decade later and with women an established asset to the scene, that they were really something to be gawped at then. National Hunt racing had for so long been an all-male domain that the very thought of lady jockeys filled many chauvinists with trepidation.

The argument raged long and hard about whether women should be allowed to race and there are still those, including some women, with firm convictions that they should not.

Luckily we live in a free world, and fortunately the women who came into NH racing on both sides of St George's Channel (for in January 1976 England followed suit) were not those seeking glamour but those who genuinely wanted to participate in the sport. Most of them had many years of point-to-point experience behind them, and that can be a particularly hazardous pastime.

They were well aware of the dangers, but being women who got a kick out of living life to the full, they relished the challenge, enjoyed the atmosphere, thrilled to the exhilaration when things went right, and picked themselves up ruefully when they did not.

When people put forward the argument that women are not so strong as men, they are generally right. But that they will be less effective on the racecourse does not follow, for what women lack in physical strength they make up in knack. There is no doubt at all that many horses *run* better for women. The women who race are those who relish a challenge and this is where what I call 'moral strength' comes into play. It is not easy to put off a determined woman, and she can tap unseen resources of strength when needs be!

Many a ham-fisted male has been carted by a tearaway when quite often a woman has the knack to hold the same horse 'in her little finger'.

The sort of strength harder for her to muster is that needed to hold together a tired horse at the end of a three-mile slog through mud. But when it comes to a tight finish, Mrs Hill and her like are not easy to beat!

Neither does this mean that they are hard, unfeminine specimens. They may give no quarter during the five minutes or so of a race, but off the race-track they mostly have smiling, womanly faces and soft natures.

That many male riders still abhor the thought of their horse kicking a female football along the ground is perfectly understandable. But women are now an accepted, albeit small, part of the scene and Ireland was to the forefront in making the historic change.

So it was on 1 January 1973 that Mrs Charmian Hill and

her horse Sundancer set out for the aptly-named Good Resolutions Plate at Fairyhouse, the Co. Meath home of the Irish
Grand National.

'Charmian Will Make History', was the bold headline em-
blazoned above Tony O'Hehir's article in the *Sunday Press* of
30 December.

'Mrs Charmian Hill, wife of a Waterford doctor, will make
racing history on Tuesday at Fairyhouse. One of the women
to be granted a licence to ride against men in bumper and
amateur chases, Mrs Hill will be the first of her sex to throw
down the gauntlet in the Good Resolutions Plate.'

There were twenty-three runners for the amateur flat race
and, it seemed, each one of her twenty-two male rivals wished
her luck as they circled down at the start.

Sundancer started an unconsidered 33–1 but struck a fine
blow for women by finishing third. Eventually he broke down
and his career was ended.

This was the start of a memorable eight years of riding
under Rules for Charmian Hill. Those who had watched her
point-to-pointing for the previous fourteen knew all about her
ability and courage, but now she was being scrutinized by a
much wider audience. And they warmed to her.

Never was her ability better demonstrated than on The
Jester, a cheap horse, which cost only £800 because he had
a 'dicky' leg. How many more Red Rums, Arkles and Dawn
Runs would there have been if only horses' legs had matched
their ability.

All too often it is the small-time owner of a moderate mare,
probably a mare none-too-well put together, who decides,
when she breaks down, to put her in foal. Thus indiscriminate
breeding takes place and at the bottom end of the scale more
moderate horses are bred, often destined after their short,
indistinguished racing careers, to end up in a riding school,
a dealing yard, or in a dog-meat can.

If a mare has won on the racecourse and proved herself it
is a different matter, as it can be hoped quite reasonably that
her ability will be passed on, and that with a careful choice
of stallion, her faults may be eradicated. Mrs Hill's Boro

Nickel, her foundation mare, although small, was well proportioned and although she eventually got a 'bit of a leg', it was not until she was eleven years old and had won seven races and placed in almost every other that she has put in foal. She was a tough mare who had remained sound for many years, with bags of ability and guts, and if all brood mares were like her, there would be less poor produce around.

The Jester's leg was not too bad and worth a gamble at the price. He would have time to strengthen up through hunting before facing the rigours of racing again.

But he proved too hot to hunt, so Mrs Hill switched him to hurdling. Even then it was with some trepidation that she set out for the Thurles Amateur handicap hurdle on Wednesday 5 October 1977, for the horse had refused to school at home and she was afraid that the same thing might happen on the course.

But there is many a good racecourse jumper, with his blood up and adrenalin flowing, who will not go near a fence at home in cold blood, and The Jester was one of them.

The Jester had a lovely front on him and from the start he jumped beautifully, obviously a hunter-chaser in the making. He not only jumped well, he galloped so strongly that he evidently had enough speed for hurdling, too, as he showed that day at Thurles.

He was soon in the lead from Even Doogles, Dark Sherry, Mullacash and Allibar (the horse who later so nearly was to give Prince Charles a feel of winning and who did give him a taste of the thrill of the sport before collapsing and dying on Nick Gaslee's Lambourn gallops).

By the third, Polar Fox, Lisa's Choice and Dark Sherry had joined in the fray behind The Jester and as they passed the stands to set out on the final circuit it was the same horses in contention.

But letting them play themselves out up front while he sat patiently behind them was leading amateur Ted Walsh on the favourite Milan Major. He had infinitely more race-riding experience than most of his rivals and he was waiting until it was time to make his move.

Mrs Hill knew that by riding a front runner she was on a hiding to nothing; if she lost she could be accused of making too much use of her horse, so she had to sit and suffer, imagining rivals waiting to pounce from behind.

Turning into the home straight, Ted began picking off his rivals like ripe plums from a tree until only The Jester was left in front of him. Then came the contentious part of the race, an incident which was to produce much long debate.

As they came to the second last flight Ted Walsh tried to come through a narrow gap on the inside. But Mrs Hill wasn't budging an inch and there was 'a bit of a scrimmage'.

The pair were locked together from there, over the last flight, and all the way to the winning post, looking inseparable. The photograph showed The Jester the winner by a head.

But he had not won yet, for a prolonged Stewards' Enquiry followed, and although they found there had been interference at the second last, and that Mrs Hill had been responsible for it, she kept the race, for disqualification could only follow if the matter had happened *after* the penultimate fence. She could be disqualified only if the stewards felt *intentional* interference or foul riding had taken place at any stage in the race.

The sporting Mrs Hill and The Jester were cheered all the way to the line, and again in the winner's enclosure.

Ted Walsh took his defeat well, declaring, 'She's the best claimer in the country!'

The Thurles race certainly caught the sportswriters' imaginations:

'Mrs Hill Shocks Thurles Punters' was the heading over Brian Fetherstonhaugh's report. He continued, 'It's not often that Ted Walsh finds a photo finish going against him in amateur races, but the champion had that unusual reverse yesterday, being beaten by a head by The Jester, ridden by grandmother Mrs Charmaine (*sic*) Hill.

'The crowd gave her a loud reception as she battled on to hold Walsh's mount, Milan Major, throughout the hectic last two furlongs.

'Milan Major had every chance, but he was not helped when The Jester came in against him going to the second last, an incident that provoked a long stewards' enquiry.

'The result was allowed to stand, however, providing the gallant Mrs Hill with her third success of the year.'

For Cliffe Noone, whose article in the *Irish Field* of 8 October was headed 'Mrs Hill's Merited Win on The Jester', it was 'what looked like being one of those really miserable rainy days' as he drove down to Thurles, but it 'turned out to be one of the most pleasant afternoons imaginable'.

He called the grandmother the hero of 'the very interesting mixed programme of NH and Flat and it really was an enjoyable day's racing'.

He described the incident between Milan Major and The Jester: 'They got a little close at the second last when Milan Major tried to poke up the inside of The Jester but Mrs Hill kept her mount going so strongly that she held the advantage to the line.'

Another report was flamboyant. Under the headline 'The Jester's Win Was No Joke' and a picture of Ted Walsh with the caption 'Beaten by a Granny!' the article said: 'When a sixty-two-year-old granny beats our top amateur Ted Walsh by a head at the end of a two-and-a-half-mile handicap hurdle and then survives a Stewards' Enquiry before being allowed to keep the race, does it suggest that our amateur races are just a harmless bit of fun, or does it underline their cut throat competitiveness?'

He described Mrs Hill as a 'quite remarkable woman and horses really do seem to run for her'.

He went on, 'At Thurles Ted Walsh, on the favourite Milan Major, was trying to come through at the second last hurdle. On the inside of Mrs Hill. He got "done".'

Milan Major's trainer, Tom Bergin, thought he should have got the race, but 'Mrs Hill certainly didn't jostle Ted Walsh – there wouldn't be too many who'd dare to – and what interference there was happened at the second last, not the last,' he said.

He cited an earlier case when a jockey had objected to the

winner for taking his ground at the second last. It was over-ruled and the rule pointed out to the objector.

Thurles was not the only time Mrs Hill was up before the Stewards. There was also an occasion in the early seventies at Punchestown when she was riding Kilbricken Money. She had ridden the horse there before not long after women were allowed to ride under Rules and she remembers thinking it was better than point-to-pointing.

The next time it was pouring with rain, and she didn't walk the course. In the race, Kilbrittin Money jumped his way into the lead but, with rain pouring into her face, Mrs Hill failed to see a marker in time and went the wrong side of it, a little matter she had to explain to the stewards. But mainly her reputation as a canny race-rider grew.

7

The Crash

There were other horses that came Charmian Hill's way during the seventies and many of them were never quite able to fulfil their undoubted promise.

Slaney Gorge was probably the first really good horse she had, but his form was inclined to be erratic. He won the Guinness Chase at Punchestown but ran poorly under Rules thereafter. He went so badly in a prestigious race at Sligo that Mrs Hill thought he must be lame, but next morning he proved demonstrably that this was not so. The Hills were staying in a Bed and Breakfast nearby when he got out of his box early in the morning and galloped so far, jumping so many fences en route, that Mrs Hill thought perhaps he would make a point-to-pointer.

He appeared to take on a new lease of life, as horses sickened of training often will after a spell of hunting, but he still had his own way of doing things. There was no way Charmian could hold him back in a point-to-point, but she relished the challenge he set and really enjoyed riding him.

He ended up winning the local Waterford point-to-point, on a tight course which meant galloping round the circuit three times.

Mrs Hill had him in her customary position on the inside and horse after horse tried to head him. But he raced so magnificently that day, winning well, that Mrs Hill decided to put him back into training.

It looked as though the spot of hunting and informal point-to-pointing had done the trick but it could never be tested: not long after he returned to training Slaney Gorge suffered a freak racing accident when he broke a hind leg between fences and had to be destroyed. It left his jockey, Paddy Keily, in tears.

The horse was insured and with the two thousand pounds pay-out she received Mrs Hill bought Yes Man which she heard of through Waring Willis, champion Irish amateur rider of 1941 and 1946 whose wins included the Ulster National. He turned out a string of good class winners from his Skryne, Tara, Co. Meath, home since turning his hand to training in 1945 and in his daughter Jessica he has one of Ireland's top lady riders.

Waring warned that Yes Man was a very 'flat-bred' horse, and Jessica was only just breaking him at the time.

Eddie Hill was in hospital after a tree fell on his back, and between visits to him Mrs Hill decided to go and look at the horse and went along to Skryne. She immediately liked what she saw and thought to herself 'this is no flat weed'. Like many other people, she finds it difficult to pinpoint why she likes a horse, but knows straight away if she does. As the horse was only being broken then, she went away and thought about it, returning a few weeks later when she was able to ride him, and eventually she bought him. It was not long before she found Yes Man was too much for her at home and, ever a realist, she sent him to Paddy Mullins.

Yes Man proved a 'real little character'. Incredibly quick on his feet, he was like a little eel and got rid of everyone who sat on him, except Mrs Hill. Before long he was ready for running in bumpers. Forever on tenterhooks, he took a fierce hold going to the start and invariably tore off in his races. Eventually Mrs Hill found she could settle him in front but, although he placed many times, he kept on getting beaten.

It was about his eighth race when he went to Killarney and at long last kept his nose in front all the way to the winning-post. It was also Mrs Hill's first win in a bumper.

It was the greatest feeling and they were so excited that when Eddie thought he had also won the jackpot he immediately suggested a mini holiday and they stayed on in Killarney relaxing for a few days. It was only on their return that Eddie discovered he had not, after all, won the jackpot.

Yes Man also won a flat race at Listowel out of the blue that year and again the following year in a quagmire after pouring rain when the other jockeys allowed Mrs Hill to lead at a very slow pace. She won easily, and was proving herself one of the most able lady jockeys riding. When she also won a hurdle race on Yes Man at Tramore she was on the crest of a wave but then Paddy Mullins felt it was time the horse was switched to chasing.

'Fine. Who's riding?' Mrs Hill asked, having stuck to flat racing and hurdling herself.

'You are,' he told his astonished elderly owner. 'He goes well for you.'

She agreed, but felt it was one of the bravest things she ever did.

Before the race she went to The Curragh to school him and that gave her the confidence she needed. It was a very windy day on the wide expanse of turf, little clouds scudding across the grey skies. In the distance lorries hurried down the road leading from Dublin to Kildare which dissects the heath. To the west were the empty grandstands and white railings standing like lonely sentinels on The Curragh racecourse, used only for flat racing and home of Ireland's premier classic, the Irish Sweeps Derby.

The schooling fences on the training part of The Curragh are well used, not only by local trainers but also by those who bring horses from many miles away. There are several sets of schooling fences of varying heights, including full size with a 'regulation' or, in English terms, open ditch.

Mrs Hill showed Yes Man the first one she was taking, turned and trotted back far enough to start her school. The clever little horse absolutely pinged the fences like an old hand and gave his intrepid rider a great feeling.

So next, in December 1979, it was the real thing at Clonmel, 'The Meadow of Honey', an ancient walled town some thirty miles south-east of Waterford in Co. Tipperary. The Comeragh

Mountains make a magnificent backcloth and in between them and the town runs the River Suir, with the racecourse tucked in between.

The race went like a dream. Coming to the 'regulation' for the last time, Mrs Hill was afraid Yes Man might be tiring, but he stood back and jumped it from nearly outside the wing.

Mrs Hill slipped her reins to the buckle, leant right back almost on to his quarters as in old-fashioned prints, landed safely, gathered up the reins and, storming into the last, galloped home a convincing winner. In the process he made history for his owner, who thus became the first woman in Irish racing to win on the flat, over hurdles and a chase, a splendid feat.

He could have been anything in the making. But the following year, in November 1980, disaster struck. It was a hurdle, this time at Thurles, and, just as Yes Man was looking like running into a place, he completely misjudged the second last. A gasp went up from the stands as he somersaulted, breaking his own neck and that of his fearless owner/rider who was pinned under him. Charmian remembers nothing of the 'Crash', as she calls it.

The crowd looked on horrified at the sight of the tiny, inert figure lying under half a ton of dead horse. Eddie could not always accompany his wife racing because of his work but he was there that day and knew at once that it was serious.

He went with his diminutive, unconscious wife, sirens wailing, to Ardkeen Hospital, Waterford, barely a mile from their home, for what was to be the start of three months in different hospitals.

Besides breaking her neck, Mrs Hill had broken ribs on both sides of her body, the horse, in rolling on her, having effectively crushed her like a steam roller. Every slight movement felt like a knife thrust in her side once she came round, to laugh or cry impossible.

The treatment for her broken neck was to place her head in an uncomfortable brace with thirty pounds of weights hanging down the back to keep her perfectly immobile; one false move and she could still be paralysed.

After two days she was flown by helicopter to a hospital in Dun Laoghaire, Dublin, which specialized in back injuries and where the staff were wonderful. She had to be turned every four hours, a laborious process, to prevent bed sores from developing.

But her problems were not over yet. Before Christmas her kidneys had packed up and she was transferred again to another hospital. She felt it was an awful place and Christmas was a subdued affair that year. She was in intensive care because of her kidneys but the staff there did not seem to understand the injury side of her problems. Mrs Hill felt thoroughly fed up and her indomitable spirits sank to an all-time low.

Eventually she was allowed out of bed, but after lying for so long she could not stand up at all, let alone walk, her knees just buckled under her.

Slowly she improved and she went back to the Dun Laoghaire hospital getting progressively more mobile. It was two months, well into January, before the last of the weights came off, but as she lay there, Mrs Hill never doubted she would race again. She would just have to buy herself a decent horse on which to make her comeback, that was all.... To race again was a goal which kept her weakened spirits alive during those long, dark weeks.

It was with a sinking heart that she then had to return to the awful hospital for more kidney treatment on a drip, but at least she was now able to move around a bit and so it did not seem quite so torturous.

It was from here that she tasted her first bit of the outside world for almost three months when she was allowed out for a weekend with her daughter Penny. At last she was able to have a bath, to wash her hair, and to feel a woman again. It was being deprived of these things which she remembers most about hospital.

At last Mrs Hill returned home, her weight down from her normal eight stones to an elfin-like six and a half stones. All her muscles had wasted away and she found herself tripping and falling frequently, no longer the tough, wiry, determined lady jockey at all.

It was still wintertime and her emaciated frame felt the cold bitterly. She spent most of each day huddled up in front of the study fire, shivering. If she had told anyone then of her intention to race again, they would have scoffed at her.

There was only one thing for it: sunshine.

'Right,' said Eddie, 'we're going to the Canaries.'

It was not the sort of place they usually went to, but then it was absolute heaven. When she first came to go in the water, however, Mrs Hill was absolutely petrified. Normally a strong swimmer, she still could not turn her head and felt like a child unable to swim. But the sun worked well and the holiday pulled her together.

It proved the turning point in her recovery, and in late April, nearly six months after the crash, Mrs Hill decided to bring in her hunter Dolly, who had missed virtually the whole season because of the accident.

She was barely strong enough to lift the saddle but the mare was grass fat and Charmian knew she would behave. To begin with she just held on to the reins and pommel like a learner, but it got her going again. It was a very brave thing to do on her own but typical of her determination. In no time at all she was wanting to exercise racehorses again and she asked Paddy Mullins if he had something nice and quiet for her. To his eternal credit he obliged though no one could have blamed him had he cried off such a responsibility, for she could still barely pull up the easiest horse.

But soon she was cantering around the grass field behind Doninga and as the wind blew into her face so her blood warmed up, and she longed to be racing again. First, she would have to find a suitable horse on which to make her comeback, and she was prepared to pay a lot more money than ever before.

This she did when purchasing Diamond Do for eight thousand guineas and within a few weeks, incredibly, the pair won a 'bumpers' race. It was a feat which earned her justifiably glowing newspaper headlines and tributes, although she was quick to praise the horse, knowing her own strength was weak and her muscles still wasted.

'I was a complete passenger,' she confessed. It really made her achievement all the greater.

Diamond Do went on to win a chase (not with Mrs Hill in the saddle) and it looked as if he was on the upgrade, although he had a funny temperament and could be a very difficult ride on the racecourse.

But then he had a fall and his jaw was broken by the hoof of a passing horse. He was unable to eat and vet Paddy Fennelly took a lot of trouble with him. He collected Diamond Do from a veterinary college and brought him back to his own home near a creamery at Callan and fed the horse on gallons of milk. In time he was able to eat grass although he still could not chew hay or oats, and he never ran again, Mrs Hill eventually selling him for 'twopence nothing'.

So again she found herself without a horse, but Diamond Do had cost a lot of money, and she had not been able to claim insurance on him, and so she spoke to her son Oliver to see if he would share a horse with her. For many years he had taken no more than a passing interest in horses, aware of them only through his mother's exploits. He had resolved since childhood, when he felt horses were rammed down his throat, to have as little as possible to do with them. But when his mother broached the subject he owed her a favour, and so he agreed to buy a horse with her, a move he was never to regret, and which brought them closer together as a family.

They agreed a maximum price of six thousand pounds and Oliver let his mother get on with the job she knew best of finding the right article. That was in October 1981, just in time for the November Sales.

Mrs Hill pored through the catalogue, looking for those horses she thought might be suitable, and marked off ten. But there was one which on paper, to her eyes, seemed outstanding, the filly by Deep Run out of an Arctic Slave mare. She was sure it would make too much money, but she ticked it as well, just in case.

8

She May Never Make
a Racehorse

On 6 November Mrs Hill set off to Ballsbridge Sales with Jack Evoy, the retired groom who for a number of years had given her a hand at the local point-to-points. Armed with her list of eleven possible horses, they looked at the first ten. One or two were quite nice, others were clearly unsuitable, but none of them really caught her eye. She left the Deep Run filly to last because she was sure it would be out of her reach, but then they made their way to box number twenty-nine. Her reaction was immediate.

'The filly just *walked* out of the box. I said to myself, "Wow, here we go," I really and truly did.' Her quick voice fills with excitement still as she recalls that first, vivid moment that she set eyes on the horse.

'It was the way she walked out, you know. She was big, not done up for the sales, and gawky.

'She trotted up and down and I could see she had the kind of temperament I needed if I was going to have her at home. She wasn't really taking any notice of all the commotion that was going on around her. Even in the ring she was calm, she wasn't worried about anything.'

Although the filly was 'unfurnished', Mrs Hill also noted that she had lovely limbs, was a superb mover beneath that gawky frame, and was built in perfect proportion. This had to be the one!

She gripped the edge of the sale ring tightly as lot twenty-nine, Mr John Riordan's Deep Run filly walked calmly into the ring. It was 10.45 a.m. The bidding began and Mrs Hill flicked her catalogue discreetly to catch the eye of auctioneer Mr David Pim.

At five thousand guineas the bidding paused. For one exciting moment Mrs Hill thought the filly would be knocked down to her for an amazing bargain sum. But Mr Pim (who also runs Anngrove Stud) was a professional at his job and soon conjured more bids out of the crowd.

Now it was getting horribly close to Mrs Hill's six thousand limit. She bid once more, at five thousand, eight hundred guineas. If anyone else put in another bid now, her limit would be exceeded. She gripped the rail tighter, hardly daring to breathe, staring earnestly at the auctioneer willing him to drop the hammer as, in what seemed an eternity, he tried in vain to procure another bid.

At last he dropped the hammer. It was over. The filly was hers.

The filly spent her first night after the sale in such a tiny, low shed at the home of her transporter that when Mrs Hill arrived to collect her she had to be coaxed to come out of it, but she was soon settling in at Belmont.

The next morning Charmian took a long, hard look at what she had bought. Sometimes you can get carried away at a sale and the next day wonder what on earth possessed you as you inspect the poor specimen now in front of you.

Not so with this one. The mare stood a good 16.2 hh (although the catalogue described her as about sixteen hands) and Mrs Hill explained in later years what took her eye: 'She is so well proportioned. The great thing about her is this: you can see a long line right from her withers down over her quarters. I remember being told ages ago that that is what makes a jumper with speed; the long curving line of her back goes smoothly down over her quarters without a demarcation line.'

After the sale she rang Oliver to tell him of their purchase, and one of the first things they did was choose a name. Penny was in training for a marathon when her brother and mother discussed the naming of the three-year-old filly by Deep Run out of Twilight Slave. She was getting up at dawn to run and so the name Dawn Run tied in beautifully, and to their delight they discovered the name was free, and so Dawn Run was registered.

Warned that the filly was barely broken in, Mrs Hill planned to wait until she had some help before riding her, so for a week she put on a saddle and bridle and took her out 'on the rope' (the lunging rein).

Then one day when she had her in the yard the filly was so quiet that Charmian put her foot in the stirrup, sat on her back and rode away. She never had any trouble with her and she was the easiest young horse she had ever come across.

Mrs Hill was already past sixty, not, one might say, an ideal age to start backing youngsters. But Dawn Run really did have an exceptional temperament. The pair of them rode around the fields surrounding their home and along the quieter roads on the outskirts of Waterford, making friends and building up mutual trust and respect.

Dawn Run was still the green school-girl but her new owner soon discovered that the big, gentle mare liked to learn about something strange quietly, not with a fight. If she saw something she didn't like she would stop stock still, rooted to the ground, until she was coaxed forward by Mrs Hill's firm but kind voice, 'Go on'. She would then accept whatever it was without further ado, and displayed no vices, never bucked or reared – a paragon for an elderly owner!

Because the mare was big, it was naturally assumed that she would need time – indeed her breeder John Riordan even offered to retain her for a year on his farm for nothing – but she learnt and developed so fast that she came to hand surprisingly quickly. She was lovely to ride, with everything in front of her, a tremendous girth and shoulder; and a walk that said it all.

Christmas came and went and at New Year Dawn Run became officially four. It was not long before the pair were doing more together, even popping over a few fences, and she began to learn to gallop. One day they were going a bit faster in a field when they came to a muddy patch that would have slowed up most horses, but Dawn Run never changed her stride or altered her rhythm. With this sort of feeling, Mrs Hill's hopes began to run high. Could this gentle mare turn out to be *the* one, the stuff that dreams are made of, the reason so many people keep trying and striving through the daily setbacks that make up racing life?

So, her preparation at home completed, it was time in the spring for Dawn Run to go to Paddy Mullins and for her promise to be put to the test on the racecourse.

Mrs Hill rang her trainer and told him how pleased she was.

'But,' she warned, 'there's just one thing; she's so placid that I'm afraid she may never make a racehorse. I don't think she'll be competitive enough.'

Paddy liked the general look of her when she arrived: she was well bred for chasing and was a decent size with good bones. After she had been with him for a few weeks and had started cantering he admired her power but her action was so high that he thought she would be a real mudlark, that she would want bottomless ground.

She was put in the care of John Clarke, himself a newly-arrived stable lad fresh from school. As she began to get racing fit, so she became a bit ticklish when she was being groomed, but most of the time she was quiet and a real good 'doer', eating well. He groomed her for half an hour each day until her coat shone. Mrs Hill came over to ride her out once or twice a week, but otherwise he rode her himself in all her work.

It was not long before she was ready for her first race, and Mrs Hill teamed up with her for the Corinthian Fillies Irish National Hunt flat race, Division 2, for four-year-olds only over two miles at Clonmel on Thursday, 27 May 1982. It was an evening meeting and this was the last race on the card at 8.30 p.m.

By this time Dawn Run was firmly registered in Mrs Hill's name. It had been the intention that she should be registered in the name of Oliver's company but Oliver found it a messy business trying to register a company with all the paperwork it involved, and the next thing he knew Dawn Run was entered for her first race and he hadn't completed it. So she ran in his mother's name and colours, which turned out for the best as it was his mother who was so well known and respected by the Irish, whereas Park Hill Developments would have meant nothing to the racing public.

There were twelve runners and Mrs Hill was the only lady rider in the race for which Ribow Mist, who finished fourth, was favourite, the winner being 7–1 shot Swinging Sovereign.

Even in her first race Dawn Run, later to become a confirmed front-runner, went straight into the lead and there she stayed for five furlongs. At halfway she was second but had slipped back to fourth five furlongs out. From there she could be expected to drop back further.

But not a bit of it! This is where, in spite of her inexperience, she showed she *was* competitive, laid back her ears, and determinedly regained the lead half a mile from home.

Mrs Hill, in the saddle, found the mare was raging. She was up in the first four, just riding round, but second time round at the top of the hill two horses came up to her, one on either side, and she laid back her ears at them, Mrs Hill gave her a smack because she thought she was going to kick them. 'And she's been exactly the same ever since, if anything comes near her she just goes, "Oh, no, not me!" ' says Mrs Hill.

Oliver watched the race with his girlfriend Vonny and saw the mare 'getting cross and putting her ears back'.

Paddy Mullins was afraid it meant she was going to be a bit madamy.

John Riordan, her breeder, was there for that first race and thought, as she was passing them all, that she had unbelievable speed.

The mare slipped back to finish eighth, but it had been a highly satisfactory introduction and had illustrated that she possessed that finest, intangible quality in a racehorse; heart.

No matter how well bred a horse is, or how much ability it possesses, it is useless if it does not have the heart to go out and win its races. The lack of it can render a blue-blood useless but with it a commoner can do well. In a horse like Dawn Run, who already had the breeding, conformation and inherent ability, it can make the good turn out excellent. Dawn Run will *not* be beaten, if she can help it! There are far fewer mares than geldings in NH racing and of those, only a handful will be any good. But when a mare is good, she is very, very good. Dawn Run is a tigress on the racecourse and in a very short time by NH standards she was to capture the hearts of racing folk more than at any time since the legendary Arkle or Red Rum.

9

The End of One Legend,
the Start of Another

If that first run showed promise, it was the second that began to put it into practice and the third that saw it materialize. Dawn Run's next race was on 17 June 1982 at Thurles, scene of Mrs Hill's triumph on The Jester over Ted Walsh and of her terrible accident with Yes Man.

She was again in the last race, the Devils Bit INH flat race for four-year-old fillies at 8.30 p.m. and there were fourteen runners.

This time Dawn Run knew she was at the races and was very excitable! There was a narrow gap out on the course after the walk from the paddock and the mare was keyed up, swinging her ample quarters from side to side, raking at the bit in an effort to get going. No longer was she the placid, quiet mare, and the race began badly for her because she was so strung up that she had a poor start and was well behind on the first circuit. When they turned into the straight for the last time she ran very wide and was lying only eighth. Deciding she had better do something to try to improve matters, Mrs Hill tapped her on the shoulder. Suddenly she found herself passing horse after horse; Dawn Run was absolutely flying down the hill.

There was no hope of catching the leaders and they finished a well beaten fourth but she had made up no end of ground, and Mrs Hill thought the mare could really be a racehorse after all. Dawn Run had given her a great 'feel', and she went home full of dreams. Dawn Run, for her part, took it in her stride, although getting stronger all the time on the gallops and becoming quite a handful in the stable for John Clarke when he was grooming her. But she never went off her feed, and remained her quiet self during the daily rest periods, head down, resting a hind leg in the straw.

Tuesday, 23 June 1982 is a day Charmian Hill will never forget. It was less than a week since Dawn Run's last run but she was improving all the time and so it was decided to run her again at Tralee.

Because there is no close season for NH racing in Ireland its year runs with the calendar from January to December, when the leading jockeys' titles are decided, but renewal of licences takes place half-way through the year on 1 July.

It was now nearly the end of June and so Mrs Hill had sent off for her renewal without a second thought. That Tuesday morning she had checked round the animals at home, now turned out to grass for the summer, and had got her kit together before pouring the coffee at the small kitchen table and settling down to sort through the day's post.

She opened the typed envelope bearing the Irish Turf Club's name nonchalantly, then stared at its contents in disbelief.

Her licence to ride was not to be renewed. No reason was given.

There were eight days left to run on her current permit. Flabbergasted, dismayed and utterly enraged, her one re-action was to fight it all the way. And she would start by showing them all something today. . . .

If this had happened when she first reapplied after her crash with Yes Man it would have been less of a bombshell, more understandable. But since then she had not only ridden but won, thanks to Diamond Do.

Mrs Hill was undoubtedly riding better than ever. When frequently pressed to say when she would retire, she always said, 'When my nerve goes.' And it hadn't gone yet.

Tralee is in Co. Kerry, that lovely, rugged south-west tip of Ireland that is associated most with holiday-makers and subsistence farming. The rollers break straight in off the Atlantic over long, sandy beaches and rocky coves. Inland the McGillycuddy Creeks rise to a height of 3,414 feet at Carrauntoohil, only a few sheep tracks crossing them. Almost the county's only main road is the Ring of Kerry and it has many tourist stops along the way. Killarney, with its breathtaking lakes and jaunting carts, is the best-known town, but for the person or family who wants to get away from it all there are plenty of opportunities. This is the land where life plods on literally at the pace of the donkeys pulling the milk carts to the creamery. This is where cloth-capped, pipe-smoking, wizened old men, and those not so old, still pass the time of day with their milk churns waiting for the 'new-fangled' milk tanker to stop by. This is where peat bogs abound, with the slow, laborious hand-cutting of it into turf sods for burning on aromatic fires in the little, white-painted thatched cottages.

From the mountains many streams run into lakes, into rivers, and on into the sea. Most of them contain trout, many of them salmon, although a disease played havoc with the stock during the seventies. And the local gillies, faces deeply tanned and wrinkled, fishing flies adorning their hats, their big, cumbersome hands surprisingly deft when it comes to tying flies, still take the visitors to the best spots, still brew their tea in a Kerry kettle over an open fire. This is the part where it is difficult to think of troubles of any sort.

Tralee is on the coast in the northern part of Co. Kerry, where the rocks and heather give way to green grass and something more than the subsistence farming of the rocky areas. Here the traditional song *The Rose of Tralee* was composed by William Mulchinock in the mid-nineteenth century, and a contest with dancing to Irish bands, takes place annually to select a beauty as the Rose of Tralee. It has a bustling port and many fine beaches.

The race meeting at Tralee in June was full more of holidaymakers there for a bet and a beer and a relaxing day out, than of die-hard racing enthusiasts.

Dawn Run had ten rivals for the Castlemaine INH flat race and again it was the last race on the evening card. This time it was open to both sexes and to five-year-olds as well as four.

That Dawn Run is not from a betting stable was illustrated by the fact that although she opened at 6–4, she drifted right out to 5–1, with four horses at shorter odds. Of the ten runners, only four had ever run before, three of them, including Dawn Run, having finished fourth on their previous outing, the other, Pako Lolo, having been second.

Dawn Run was raring to go and so was her infuriated owner. There was no question of getting a bad start this time, and they quickly went into the lead and stayed there. She was in fact headed briefly by the joint-favourite Espeut just after half-way but Dawn Run would have none of it. Three furlongs out both Pako Lolo and Espeut came through to dispute the lead, but Dawn Run saw them off. . . .

Mrs Hill was as determined as her mount, and they galloped home a length clear of Espeut. It might not have been anything to write home about, but any win is always exciting for the owner. As far as the general public was concerned it was just a modest £692-to-the-winner contest, the type that any of Paddy's horses could be expected to score in, and Mrs Hill, far from accepting that this would be her last winner, was quite determined that she would get back her licence and ride again.

Her win on Dawn Run certainly seemed a timely slap in the Stewards' faces for their decision and she mustered plenty of support in her campaign to ride again.

She was livid, and said so to all and sundry in a shrill voice, and she called the Irish Turf Club's attitude 'archaic'. She had ridden winners and was capable of winning more.

Following their letter refusing to renew her permit, Mrs Hill protested in no uncertain terms. Why, she wanted to know, when she had bought two horses (Diamond Do and Dawn Run) to ride herself and had won on both of them, were they refusing her? She supported her appeal with a petition, and among the signatories was Ted Walsh. He called her a game woman and declared she was doing no harm to anybody, causing no interference, and was a lot better than many other amateurs.

The reply came thus: 'Your letter of 25 June has been placed before the Stewards. I very much regret having to inform you that the decision as conveyed to you in my letter of 21 June has been confirmed. The Stewards are not prepared to grant you a Permit to ride in INH flat races. Yours sincerely, Michael Keogh, Registrar.'

So the actual reason was never given, but the clue lies in a supremely polite and courteous letter from the same official to Mrs Hill dated 7 November 1977, nearly five years earlier, when Mrs Hill's application to ride in races open to professional jockeys was turned down.

It said: 'Thank you for your letter of 1 November. It was with the greatest reluctance that the Stewards declined to grant you permission to ride your own horses in professional NH races.

'Your experience and ability are already a matter of record and don't need to be related here. It is not usual for the Stewards of the Governing Bodies to advance reasons for the withholding or refusal of Licences but your letter in my opinion deserves an answer, and compels me to raise, with the greatest respect, the question of your age.

'You must accept, as fact, that the Stewards would not grant a Licence under INHS Rules to a professional rider of similar age, and to accede to your request would be a contradiction of accepted policy. While I fully understand your particular position, the original decision must stand.'

This Mrs Hill accepted, contenting herself to riding in amateur races only and she could see no reason why this could not continue now.

For Dr Hill it was secretly something of a relief. He was glad for his sake but sorry for her. She had had terrible accidents hunting and racing and although he always encouraged her racing and point-to-pointing, he knew they were dangerous sports.

So it was not after one of her falls, but after a splendid victory on Dawn Run no less that Mrs Hill's licence was taken away.

In fairness, one cannot envy the Stewards faced with making such a decision. On the one hand they had a perfectly fit, able, amateur rider; on the other, they had to take into account her great age (for a jockey) and their 'responsibility to her and the public'.

So it was that for Dawn Run's next race she had a male jockey in the saddle, the youngest of trainer Paddy Mullins' four sons, Tom.

10

Down in Co. Kilkenny
There is a Trainer

The Mullins are a remarkable family. If Dawn Run had an amateur breeder and amateur owner/rider, she had a true professional in her trainer. There cannot be many families which share the Mullins' record: Paddy, his wife Maureen, and their five children Sandra, Willie, George, Tony and Tom have *all* ridden winners!

Paddy Mullins was born on 28 January 1919, the son of William Mullins who farmed land adjacent to Paddy's present home at Doninga, Gorsebridge, Co. Kilkenny.

Leaving the old Co. Wexford town of New Ross by a drawbridge over the River Nore where it is wide and flat before it joins the River Suir, one heads up a steep, narrow valley of a tributary towards Graiguenamanagh in Co. Kilkenny. The landscape soon becomes a ravine with heather and bracken on the hills and the river winding deeply below. It is rugged and wild and very rough and windy going on towards Gorsebridge where the land flattens out into a fertile plain. A little corn grows but it is mostly small fields with large, unclipped hedges on top of stone-faced banks, a few sheep dotted about.

Gorsebridge itself is a fairly typical unlovely small Irish town, with an unsightly stone quarry and a huge, ugly, castellated decrepit building. It is home of a big feed mill; of well-known horse and pony sales; and of Ireland's leading NH trainer, Paddy Mullins.

71

Doninga, his home, is a long, low white farmhouse made ever brighter in the dull grey winter months by colourful red and orange berries covering the entrance wall just off the road, barely a mile out of Gorsebridge.

A cheerful fire usually glows at one end of the long, low sitting room which is tidy and tastefully furnished, with comfortable easy chairs. Racing pictures and photographs adorn the walls, including a very happy Maureen winning her one and only race, and some favourite paintings by the artist Snaffles. A few racing trophies, including some Waterford Crystal, are dotted around and a set of twelve plates with pictures of all the family members winning are on a table.

Almost everywhere one goes in Ireland, Paddy's training is praised and with fifty or so horses, the biggest NH yard in Ireland, his record simply stands for itself. He knows when it is right to run a horse or not.

The main stable yard is right behind the house, with more boxes which were completed early in 1985 to one side.

'I said I wouldn't build any more,' Paddy smiles ruefully, 'but once you start turning owners away, they won't come back.'

The stables built up gradually over the years after Paddy took over the licence from his father in 1953 having been his assistant for thirteen years before that. In only fairly recent times has the stable reached the upper echelons, establishing a high reputation with many winners of big races both on the flat and jumping.

Paddy grew up with hunting being a natural part of life and he enjoyed following the Kilkenny hounds on a variety of ponies, able to take his own line without fear of barbed wire or electric fencing. He joined the Pony Club, and tried his hand at showjumping just as many another kid of his day, until there was a natural progression into the local point-to-points.

He won about twenty-five and was also successful fourteen times under Rules, scoring on the flat, over hurdles and in chases, all as an amateur.

Breeding, rearing and training all followed on, and he still derives a lot of pleasure from breeding, keeping up to half a dozen mares.

He has always had a mixed yard of jumpers and flat horses, and he finds it particularly lucrative to sell a good filly for the flat.

'They are like gold dust,' he says. 'I've sold a few and it all helps.'

In his early years, Paddy could be described as a small-time trainer, and one feels there is a hidden conflict within him between preferring it that way, out of the limelight, but yet having the perfectionist's wish to keep on improving.

The only drawback for a man of his nature to the success that the latter brings is the accompanying attentions of the Press.

'I hate publicity,' he says, his chin almost on his chest, his hands grasped tightly round his locked knees. 'They all talk through their pockets.'

Paddy is a non-betting man, and his is a non-gambling stable.

'I've no time for the Press at all,' he suddenly becomes animated. 'I never back my own horses, and only very occasionally have a few pounds on others for interest.'

His reason is simple: 'Because it's nearly impossible to win.'

Nevertheless, his aversion to publicity is unfortunate, because his is a very public profession. 'What the Press says does worry me a bit,' he says, looking up from under the lock of silvery grey hair falling across one eye. Certainly Paddy is a very sensitive man.

Only when he shows someone the horses in his yard does he unwind a little and start to relax as he is with the animals he loves, none more so than Dawn Run who has a box on her own, almost facing the back door of the house. It is very big and light and airy and filled with deep straw.

There are about fifteen lads in the yard, in addition to all four of the Mullins' sons. Of the four, only Tony is professional, because he is the only one who can do a low weight. It was Tony's good fortune, Paddy believes, that William was heavier, because he is probably just as good a jockey, and

Dawn Run

particularly capable over fences. William point-to-pointed for many years and is an excellent judge of pace.

William is the eldest son, and also the only one to have spent any length of time away from home, having stayed for a valuable period in Australia as assistant trainer to Neville Beg. Now he is assistant trainer to his father.

He went on to make his first ride at the NH Festival at Cheltenham a winning one on Hazy Dawn in 1982, and two years later he did it again, winning the four-mile NH Chase on Macs Friendly. In the year in between he won the Liverpool Foxhunters on Ath Cliath (which is Gaelic for Dublin) as part of the first ever all-Irish combination of horse, owner, trainer and rider to win it.

George is the second son and although another thoroughly capable amateur rider, the farm is his main interest, running both the home farm, where all the training takes place, and Paddy's other farm three miles away. He rides out once every day, then gets on with the farm work while the other brothers ride out at least another two lots. George's riding career may seem a little overshadowed by his brothers, yet he has ridden getting on for twenty winners himself.

Tom is the youngest, and he has the enviable record of being unbeaten on Dawn Run. It was he who rode her in her remaining two flat races after Mrs Hill was forced to quit.

The Mullins' daughter Sandra, the eldest of the children, is married to Dublin businessman Peter McCarthy, and she still visits the family home most weekends. It was in 1982 that she had about five rides on the flat, winning the Rose of Tralee ladies' race and finishing third in a one-off invitation charity race, the Ceville Lodge Stakes, for trainers' wives and daughters at local Gowran Park.

This was the race won by her mother Maureen on her only ride on a professional racecourse and she did it in style, too, storming clear on Razzo Forte to win by six lengths. It need not have been such a surprise for as Miss Doran before she was married, Maureen was an able point-to-point rider.

Third son Tony's career almost ended the day it began. In 1979, at the age of seventeen, he had his first ride in a

74

point-to-point on a horse called Creidim. It was the local
Kilkenny Hunt meeting, held on the inside of Gowran Park
racecourse. Tony, who by all accounts had been a bit of a
devil-may-care in the Pony Club, was helpless in what happened, for the horse died in mid-air and landed heavily on
top of his slim young rider. Tony's leg was so badly broken
that he was unable to ride again for over a year.

Yet by 1982 he was leading claiming rider (the equivalent
of an apprentice on the flat), and in 1983, his first as a senior
rider, he finished third in the jockeys' table to Frank Berry.
One year later he tied for the title, having at one time been
five winners clear of Frank Berry. The mishap on Tony's
debut only made him more determined than ever and, as I
write, he has yet to have another really serious injury.

Besides Tony and his amateur brothers, the yard has Peter
Kavagnagh as second jockey and several of the lads have
'boys' licences.

The rides seem to be sorted out amicably between the
brothers with no arch-rivalry, probably because Paddy holds
the reins and they all respect his judgement.

For a mother, to have a racing son can be a nerve-racking
experience; to have all four riding regularly might be a night-
mare. Maureen is very much a part of the business set-up, as
well as looking after the home and family. She is a most able
and efficient secretary, one of the things that keeps her busiest
is the almost constant ringing of the telephone.

Paddy says, 'When the boys were growing up, I never
dreamt that they would all ride. But they don't want to do
anything else and so we have to live with it, although people
think we're daft!'

The sons have all had strictly equal opportunities, and the
horses have certainly turned out well for them. To maintain
a degree of independence, all four indulge in a little buying
and selling in their own right. 'The horses have been good
to us,' Paddy says warmly. 'I wouldn't wish for any other
life.'

One of the best mares he ever trained was Height
O'Fashion, remembered for some epic struggles against Arkle,

running him to a neck once when receiving *three stone* of weight. (When they first met four years before in a handicap hurdle, she had to give him twenty-three pounds.) She was also second to him in the Irish Grand National. These races came after she had left Paddy who never raced her against the great horse, but he did win twelve races with her, including the Irish Cesarewich.

Paddy lets a training programme evolve round a given horse without hard and fast advance plans. But of one thing he is sure. He will never run Dawn Run in the Grand National.

In fact he had never had a runner in the Grand National until 1985, when Tony Mullins led for some way on Dudie. He trained Nicholas Silver earlier in the same season that he won, and he had formerly trained Andy Pandy who set up a long lead before falling in the big race.

'Either I haven't had the right horses or the owner hasn't wanted it,' he says without a tinge of regret. This is a man who has a soft spot for his charges.

'I let the horse tell me what it is capable of. My aim is to do the best I can with them.'

Most of the galloping is done in the fields around Doninga and, as with most Irish trainers, much of the schooling is done either on the Curragh or after racing on courses. Indeed, some racecourses occasionally stage an all-schooling day, split into sessions over different distances.

And so it was on 31 July 1982, with the ground hard and Mrs Hill having failed in her bid to have her licence renewed, that eighteen-year-old Tom Mullins teamed up with Dawn Run for her final bumpers at Galway.

11

This is Some Mare

Eddie and Charmian Hill drove from their south-eastern corner of Waterford across the central plains of Ireland to its rugged west coast for the festival meeting at Galway. It was not an easy drive, for Mrs Hill felt petulantly resentful that she could not be riding her horse herself and the feeling of injustice was only rubbed in further as she could see scores of holiday-makers enjoying themselves in their chosen pastimes, be it swimming from the sandy beaches or feeding the wild ponies on the edge of rocky Connemara where they picnicked.

Just inland the little grass fields were divided by a criss-cross of dry-stone walls which made endless jumping opportunities for followers of the popular Galway Blazers hunt in winter, a pack which is something of a tourist attraction in itself. Indeed, were it not for the American, English and German visitors who frequently outnumber the local subscribers the pack, founded in the early nineteenth century, would be hard pressed to keep going.

The Galway races were a part of the week-long Galway Festival and so again it was a holiday crowd that teemed in. Hard ground had produced small fields and Mrs Hill was afraid it would be too firm for her mare, yet Dawn Run and Tom Mullins coasted in from their three rivals, showing for the first time another part of her versatility.

But the victory left a hollow pit in Mrs Hill's stomach, for all she wanted was to be out there partnering her mare herself, and so the couple packed their bags and flew off to California for a holiday.

It meant missing Dawn Run's next engagement, but since this was the Sean Graham Haversnack at Tralee, a valuable flat race in which she stood virtually no chance against classier flat race rivals, it did not seem too important.

When the Hills arrived at the Californian home of friends of Oliver they found a drinks party was in full swing.

'There's a telegram for you but it doesn't seem to make much sense,' their hosts told them, and introduced them to the other guests.

Mrs Hill was dying to see what the telegram said, but had to make polite conversation until she felt she could slip out. 'DAWN RUN WALKS THE HAVERSNACK' the telegram read. It made wonderful sense to Mrs Hill but no wonder it left the Californians confounded!

Dawn Run did not run again until 13 November, in another flat race, the Leopardstown November Extel handicap. It was a disaster. Mrs Hill blamed herself for what happened. Paddy was away on holiday and she decided to see what would happen if Dawn Run was held up. But, like many a lady, Dawn Run likes to have her own way. Her resentment at being restrained was obvious. In poor Pat Gilson's hand, a stable jockey, she put her head up and hated every moment, trailing in last but one of the seventeen runners. It is the only bad race she ever ran. Leopardstown was not '*le petit* Chantilly' with its luxurious standards for Charmian Hill that day. It mattered not that it was Ireland's finest racecourse, with a magnificent grandstand overlooking the broad sweep of turf in front and attractive tree-line paddock at the back, a glass floor enabling those on the terrace to look down into the hubbub of the weighing room. All she could take in was the sight of her lovely mare trailing in last but one after three good wins in a row.

For the record, it was won by a short head by Gallant Royal from Street Angel with Potato Merchant third. And that dreadful race was to be her last on the flat that year. She was now considered ready to embark upon the next stage of her career, hurdling, both Paddy and Mrs Hill believing this simply to be a stepping-stone to what she was bred for, chasing. She schooled well at Doninga, but that is a very different matter to what she had to face in Division 2 of the Kilwarden maiden hurdle for four-year-olds only over two miles at Naas on Saturday, 27 November in heavy going, for there were twenty-nine runners. There could hardly be a more frenetic, noisy, bustling and frightening introduction for a huge bunch of maiden hurdlers. Yet, with all credit to the various trainers and jockeys, especially bearing in mind the heavy ground, no fewer than twenty-eight runners completed the course in Division 1 and all twenty-nine in Dawn Run's.

The mare, with a little jumping experience at home under Mrs Hill, and the serious schooling at Mullins', took to hurdling like the proverbial duck to water. This time she had another stable jockey, Peter Kavanagh, in the saddle, and was 5–1 joint favourite.

Only three horses had measurable previous hurdling form; Bridge Street had been fourth and finished seventh in this race; Ten Below, also fourth last time, on this occasion came tenth; and Dawn Run's stable companion Pariglit, ridden by Tony Mullins, who had been third last time, now finished fourteenth.

By half-way the huge pack began to take shape and Dawn Run was prominent; three flights from home she was second and then she disputed the running. But she 'found no extra' approaching the last and she finished a satisfactory fourth.

Seskin Bridge, ridden by Frank Berry and owned by the President of Ireland, Dr Hiliary, was the second favourite and scored by a decisive five lengths in spite of swerving right two out and making a mistake at the last. Outsider Ardgosta beat the co-favourite, By The Way, by a short head for second place and four lengths behind these came Dawn Run.

It was a creditable enough start and she was taken next to Navan on 20 December where the uphill finish and heavy ground would test her out for stamina.

The opposition for the nineteen-runner Blackhills Maiden Fillies' Hurdle was not great, and Dawn Run started at odds-on of 4–6. Next in the betting was Rositess, at 6–1, who finished third.

This was the first time that Tony Mullins teamed up with the mare. She did not forge off in front but was always well placed, disputing the lead early on and soon the big field was well strung out along the back straight, where Dawn Run lay in third.

As they turned for home, with two flights of this delightful Irish course left, she took over the lead. Determined Angel lived up to its name, challenged hard, and actually headed her before the last. But the effort left her a spent force. Dawn Run mustered more reserves and stayed on to a five-length victory. Mrs Hill was delighted.

She might not have beaten much but the way she did it was enough to begin formulating bigger ideas. A crack at the Findus Beefburger Hurdle at the Leopardstown Christmas meeting would be her next run, then, who knows, she might be able to cross the water for a go at one of Cheltenham's top novice hurdle events. It was early days to be thinking like that but, well, dreams are free and, as the song says, if you don't have a dream, how are you going to have a dream come true?

A maiden four-year-old fillies' hurdle worth £996 is a very different thing from an all age, either sex sponsored hurdle worth £5,260 to the winner at Leopardstown, whence Dawn Run was routed for the Findus Beefburger only eight days after her modest little win at Navan.

Her starting price of 12–1 reflected this very fact. But it was the day when the real potential of Dawn Run began to show itself. It was the time when she really began her now famous way of running 'Made all'. It was also the first time she met Buck House, whose path she was subsequently to cross several times.

The favourite was Dawn Run's stable companion, Castletown House, ridden by William Mullins and only three of the runners started at longer odds than Dawn Run. At two miles two furlongs, it meant there were nine instead of the usual eight flights to jump which, coupled with the yielding ground, would put a premium on stamina.

For Eddie and Charmian Hill it was stupendously exciting, for as the tapes went up the mare went directly into her long stride with her ears pricked, jumping superbly.

William Mullins on Castletown House did his best to keep in touch but was beaten by the time they turned into the home straight and finished sixth.

As Dawn Run headed for home, clearly enjoying every minute, Buck House was close on her heels and challenged strongly as they approached the last.

Here Dawn Run made what was regrettably to become another of her landmarks: a mistake at the last. Whether it was carelessness on her part, nervousness on the part of her rider (unlikely, for it happened equally with Jonjo O'Neill and Tony), or just a lack of concentration, it was an unfortunate habit to get into and one that would have cost a lesser horse several races.

But for Dawn Run it just made settling down to the business of running for home that much more intense. After all, this horse Buck House was throwing down the gauntlet, and that wouldn't do!

Mysterious Arthur, who had been hampered during the race, also put in a spirited challenge and, coming out of the pack seemingly from nowhere, was Anaglogs Pet.

In the end the mare beat Buck House by a length and a half, with Mysterious Arthur and Anaglogs Pet only one length and a neck further back.

Now Mrs Hill could really begin to dream. This was some mare. Dawn Run's breeder was there that day. It was the day Paddy Mullins had, in all sincerity, rated the mare's chances at nil, but Mr Riordan had nevertheless got his bet on – £10 each way at 14–1 – and enjoyed the thrill just as much as if she were still his own.

Cheltenham in March was now more than an idle dream, more than a distinct possibility, it was now a positive plan. Which race it would be would depend on her remaining 'prep' races. The two-and-a-half-mile Sun Alliance might suit as she was bred to stay, but she was also entered for the two mile Waterford Crystal supreme novices hurdle.

Dawn Run would not quite be Mrs Hill's first runner at Cheltenham: she once had a horse in a hunter chase there, 'a million years ago', but it fell at the water, an obstacle not used in Irish chases.

Perhaps Dawn Run could improve on the record.

12

Cheltenham's Challenge

To have a runner at Cheltenham is many an owner's dream, much as, for others, it is to have a horse in the Grand National. One is the blue riband of steeplechasing, the other the most famous, or infamous, horse-race in the world.

Not only does the National Hunt Festival at Cheltenham in the third week of March contain all the championship races, from the Cheltenham Gold Cup and the Champion Hurdle to the *Daily Express* Triumph Hurdle for four-year-olds and, the hunting fraternity's top accolade, the Cheltenham Foxhunters, but it is also, by tradition, three days of intense rivalry between the English and the Irish. It is, if you like, when each puts its best goods on display in their respective shop windows.

The Festival frequently coincides with St Patrick's Day, 17 March, just to add to the flavour and fervour, and every other voice in the huge crowd, it seems, has an Irish accent. Dozens of Irish priests, sporting their dog collars, come over, and many others will be wearing shamrocks.

Although Ireland has less racing and fewer horses than England, it is steeped in even older racing history and the tradition of producing the world's best steeplechasers has continued from that first race from the steeple of Buttevant Church to the spire of St Leger in Co. Cork in 1752, to the present day. The spa town of Cheltenham had flat racing in 1815, and the first running of the Cheltenham Gold Cup was a flat race over three miles, in 1819. The races then were on the top of Cleeve Hill and moved to their present site at Prestbury Park in 1831. For a time they prospered, until the coming of a new evangelical age and, to Cheltenham, of the Reverend (later Dean) Francis Close. He belonged to the 'anti-smoking, anti-drinking, anti-anybody-having-any-fun' brigade, and, a great orator, his influence soon spread far and wide. He used his immense power of speech to sway the masses away from the 'evils' of gambling and racing. His rhetoric gained power so that in 1829 his followers staged a demonstration on the course and the following year the grandstand was burnt down.

So the new course, in that beautiful bowl below Cleeve Hill, and its splendid grandstand capable of accommodating seven hundred and declared the best in the land, fell victim to the new Victorian morals of Dean Close and his like, and within a few years flat racing had disappeared altogether.

But waiting in the wings, as it were, was the supremely sporting sport of steeplechasing. Its passage was still not without interruption, for in 1854 the new owner of Prestbury Park refused to allow the racing there. Different sites had to be found around and about for the Grand Annual Meeting, but its significance in the calendar diminished until at the end of the century, with Dean Francis Close already dead, racing petered out at Cheltenham altogether for a few years.

Slowly it began again, and what was to prove the beginnings of the National Hunt Festival as we now know it, was held over two days in April 1902, thanks to a new owner who actively encouraged steeplechasing. Six years later the Cheltenham Steeplechase Company was formed and by 1914 the new stands – replaced only in the seventies – were completed.

After the First World War, when the racecourse buildings were used as a hospital, the Festival grew from strength to strength and in 1923 it became a three-day meeting.

Until then, the four-mile National Hunt Chase was probably the meeting's most prestigious race, but 1924 saw the inaugural running of the Cheltenham Gold Cup then, as now, an opportunity for the country's best staying chasers to meet on level terms. Only the introduction in 1983–4 of a five-pound allowance for mares has slightly altered it.

Since that first Gold Cup win by Dick Rees on Red Splash, the Gold Cup has produced some marvellous winners: Easter Hero in 1929 and 1930: the era of Miss Dorothy Paget's five-times winner Golden Miller from 1932–6 and some of his duels with Thomond; Tom Dreaper's Prince Regent (it was a long time before he could eventually concede that, twenty years later, the world's greatest chaser, Arkle, which he also trained, really was the better); Cottage Rake who won for Vincent O'Brien three times from 1948–50; the mare Kerstin, one of few of her sex to bear comparison with Dawn Run, in 1958; the gutsy Mandarin in 1962; the mighty Mill House in 1963 only to be eclipsed by the mightiest Arkle from 1964–6; the headstrong The Dikler in 1973 the year after the last successful mare, Ireland's Glencaraig Lady; the enigmatic Captain Christy in 1974; the ill-fated Averton in 1979, three weeks before he was killed in the Grand National, a tragic reward for the trainer's decision to run a horse of this calibre in the biggest 'lottery'; Silver Buck, the biggest National Hunt money earner until Dawn Run, in 1982, and in 1984 the exciting, dour Burrough Hill Lad trained by Jenny Pitman.

This is the race that inspires the greatest emotion and pleasure to steeplechasing followers just to watch the world's finest chasers pitting their wits against each other and the elements, the steep Cheltenham hills and the black birch fences, running their hearts out up that final gruelling hill to see who is truly the best – and bravest.

The success of the first Gold Cup was such that the executive soon instigated a similar event to prove who was the season's best hurdler, and so in 1927 the Champion Hurdle came into being to produce winners such as: Brown Jack in 1928: National Spirit 1947–8; Hattons Grace 1949–51; Sir Ken 1952–4; Persian War 1968–70; Bula 1978; Monksfield 1979; Night Nurse 1977 and Sea Pigeon 1980–81. Of the Champion Hurdlers, only a handful have ever attempted the Gold Cup double and, to date, none has succeeded. Night Nurse came the closest when in 1981 he was second to his stable companion Little Owl. Sea Pigeon and Bula also made brave attempts.

Nevertheless, the Irish, almost to a man, confidently expect that situation to change in the near future, and that the horse to do so will be a mare, no less!

When the Hill boys were at Dean Close, Eddie and Charmian Hill were frequent visitors, often spending a few days' holiday which invariably included visiting Cheltenham races. They found a convenient and congenial guest house in which to stay, the Cotswold Grange in Pitville Circus Road, only twenty minutes walk from the racecourse, which meant they could often be back after the Festival while drivers were still sitting in a queue, and it became virtually a second home. They were made to feel welcome by the proprietors Brian and Grace Weaver and Sarah and Peter Harris, all part of the same family, and they became friends with other guests who would stay there annually for the Festival.

When they came back in 1983 to have a runner a major seven million pound modernization of Cheltenham racecourse had taken place. The original stands had come to the end of their natural life and it was not only the British racing public who were expressing a growing demand for more luxurious facilities, but especially companies, many of whom were increasingly using racing as a means of entertaining clients or running company-owned horses.

Apart from the new grandstand, complete with Tote facilities, bars and toilets at every level, the biggest innovation was the re-siting and re-designing of the paddock and weighing-room areas. The new paddock was set in a semi-amphitheatre, the steps rising from it on three sides to give spectators a good view. The public got a much better view of the horses returning after a race, too, because instead of disappearing behind the buildings they were routed in front of the stands and through the crowds back to the paddock. It all added to the unique atmosphere of Cheltenham, something that is there even on ordinary race days and which during the Festival, has to be experienced to be believed. It is one intangible quality that television cannot transmit to armchair viewers.

One of the sensible thoughts behind the redevelopment was

that the buildings should be suitable for non-racing functions, and so it is not unusual on a race day to find little bits of confetti on the ground, remnants from a wedding reception in the banqueting hall.

So Cheltenham has come a long way since it was the scourge of Dean Francis Close – and the school which bears his name is still thriving, too, the two happily co-existing in a more liberal age. The school in fact became something of a pioneer when it became co-educational in 1972, taking in not only day girls but girl boarders, too, something of which Dean Close would hardly have approved.

And so it was in 1983 that it was decided to make the Sun Alliance Novices' Hurdle Dawn Run's Cheltenham target. It would be a highly competitive event over two and a half miles to open the card on Wednesday 16 March, the second day of the Festival.

For such a prestigious event Mrs Hill felt she should have a more experienced jockey than Tony Mullins, who was only twenty, but at the same time, being fiercely patriotic, she was determined to have an Irish jockey.

'We have as good jockeys as anyone, and it might be the only time I have a horse good enough for Cheltenham, so I want the best available,' she reasoned and set about finding who could ride her mare.

13

The Young Pretender

The ride on Dawn Run was offered to Frank Berry but he opted for the favourite, Ballinacurra Lad, so it was another Irishman 'Big Ron' Barry who had the leg up on Dawn Run in the Sun Alliance novice hurdle of 1983, a race which can often prove a pointer to future Champion hurdlers.

Twenty-seven went to post; Tony Mullins was on Mrs Playfair who finished tenth. Because of Dawn Run's known dislike of being hemmed in, Mrs Hill suggested Ron take her round on the outside. Afterwards, he felt that if he had known the mare beforehand he would have won. As it was, she was far from disgraced showing, in particular, her own special brand of gameness.

As was now usual, she set off in front of the huge pack and stayed there for two miles until headed only by the eventual winner, Sabin du Loir, but then she fought back with such tenacity and tremendous courage up the Cheltenham hill that many a punter noted her name as one for the future.

Not only punters either, for it was after this race that Mrs Hill received an offer of fifty thousand pounds for the mare.

It was a tempting moment, representing a huge profit, and Mrs Hill was afraid her son and part-owner Oliver might need the money.

Luckily he agreed not to sell her, for by now Mrs Hill had a feeling about her, and she was improving by leaps and bounds with every race.

Sabin du Loir was trained by Michael Dickinson at the meeting he made his own. His Badsworth Boy also won the next race, the Queen Mother Champion Chase, but it was the following day's Cheltenham Gold Cup that wrote him into the record books with the astonishing feat of having trained all the first five home. Bregawn was the winner, followed by Captain John, Wayward Lad, Silver Buck and, because of the unprecedented feat, even the fifth placed Ashley House was allowed to unsaddle in the winner's enclosure!

Dawn Run returned home in the finest fettle, and ate up well. She rolled in the deep straw and shook herself, completely relaxed. It was decided to return to England for the Liverpool Grand National meeting to run in the Page Three novice hurdle over the extended trip of two miles and five furlongs. The ground was unusually soft for the quick-drying Aintree soil and Dawn Run started 7–2 joint-favourite with Military Band for the thirteen-runner, four thousand pounds race.

The venture not only proved a memorable one for Dawn Run and the Hills, but that particular week was the stuff dreams are made of for the Mullins family.

It began with a wide-pronged double on Thursday, 7 April with William becoming part of the first all-Irish combination to win the Liverpool Foxhunters, the amateur's Grand National. This is run over two miles and six furlongs of the Grand National course itself and one can have nothing but admiration for the Corinthians, men and women, who tackle these awesome fences.

Young Tom Mullins, meanwhile, was back at Thurles, winning on Pass the Plate. George Mullins was in Australia as an assistant trainer at the time, so that just left Tony to continue to uphold the family honours – which he did in style.

The way in which Dawn Run won the Page Three was pure pleasure to watch. It is not all that often you really see a horse pricking its ears in a race. Sometimes a bold horse will do so as he sees the next fence and goes for it like a tiger; or a good winner, eased as it approaches the line, will prick its ears when it feels the pressure come off; but more often a horse will gallop with its ears roughly in line with its head, or loose and semi-cocked. But one of the features about Dawn Run is her abundant love of her task, shown not only by her guts but also by her gaily pricked ears.

The Page Three could not have gone more smoothly for her. It was a smaller field than at Cheltenham and although she was carrying top weight (and it was only her second run in a handicap hurdle) she was soon at the head of affairs.

Only Military Band, the co-favourite, tried to go with her; that lasted as far as the third flight after which Dawn Run surged on in her inimitable style while her co-favourite eventually pulled up. On she galloped and although Thurston looked a challenger as they turned for home, the mare was only toying with him. She surged on to a breathtaking ten-length victory, only four others toiling home in her wake, including the third-placed Amarach who she was to meet in much closer circumstances a few months later.

While Tony was enjoying himself in photo session with the Page Three pin-up girl at the trophy presentations afterwards, his father was not being drawn as to whether or not the mare would run again the next day.

Hungry newsmen made quite a meal of this, for it was no novice race in which she was engaged on Grand National day, but the Sun Templegate which was to be contested by the new Champion Hurdler Gaye Brief and the previous year's Champion, For Auction, no less.

'I'll see how she is in the morning,' Paddy told waiting reporters, 'but she didn't have a hard race today.'

That was no doubt true, but nevertheless she had galloped further than usual and in testing ground. Clearly the newsmen did not approve.

Journalist Michael O'Farrell put it bluntly: 'Brave as Dawn Run is, she does look outclassed among this field which includes last month's Champion Hurdle 1–2–3.'

In fact, the Hills did not really expect her to run back the next day and Oliver returned to his business in Dublin. He went into a pub at lunchtime, turned on the television and there she was.

Paddy had checked her at six in the morning, found she

had eaten up every oat and was raring to go, so he let her take her chance. This shrewd trainer is seldom proved wrong, but even he must have been surprised by the performance she put up.

There were just six runners for the event, again over two miles and five furlongs, and Dawn Run was the youngest. Gaye Brief was, of course, of the highest class, but the others were hardly duffs, either. The Champion was an 11–8 favourite, For Auction 3–1, Boreen Prince 4–1, Broadsword, who had finished fourth in the Champion, was at 7–1, A Kinsman was the outsider at 33–1 and the 'schoolgirl' of the party, Dawn Run, was little considered at 12–1, having been available at 16–1. This gives illustration enough between the class of the two races and is probably an indication that few punters had confidence in her doing so well on two consecutive days.

What transpired was one of Dawn Run's most memorable races, and certainly her greatest in defeat. Dawn Run was now well and truly into her pattern of running and her five rivals were content to let the outsider slip along in front.

Back on the course twenty-three hours after her facile victory in the Page Three, Dawn Run was obviously loving every minute again. This was fun! It was a clear answer to those who thought it terrible to run her again so quickly, and against the best in the land.

Incredibly, as they turned for home, only the Champion Gaye Brief was in touch with her. Already she had galloped former champion For Auction and Broadsword into the ground.

Gaye Brief moved up to Dawn Run's quarters and the mare lost a vital length with a mistake at the third last. Going into the last, the favourite took over the lead and it was all over. Or was it? Instead of forging further ahead for the expected easy victory, there was this mare nagging away, determined not to be beaten at all, even by the Champion! Dawn Run ran on so doggedly that she passed the post only one length behind. Incredibly, the remaining top hurdlers trailed in way behind. For Auction was *twenty lengths* back in third, five more to Broadsword, Boreen Prince was a distance behind him, and twenty-five lengths behind him came A Kinsman.

Charmian Hill was stunned: quite overcome. To be such a close second in those conditions was as good as winning, for sure! Another few strides and she felt Dawn Run would have got up.

Mercy Rimell, the winner's trainer, was quoted as saying that her jockey Richard Linley looked over the wrong shoulder. But to most spectators, Gaye Brief did not look to have that much in reserve. It was to be the start of a protracted duel of words concerning the two horses.

For Mrs Hill, it was suddenly the realization that hers could be the horse to become the first to win a Champion Hurdle and Gold Cup, even though it was early days yet. Paddy, ever more cautious, told reporters, now eager to glean all they could about this extraordinary mare, that she was 'unlikely to have the speed for a Champion Hurdle' and would go chasing the next year.

Two years later, he smiles coyly and says, 'Well, maybe I could have said that.'

The Press was ecstatic. The *Sporting Life* stated simply, 'As expected, Gaye Brief followed up his Champion Hurdle victory by taking the Templegate Hurdle, but it was the runner-up Dawn Run who stole the limelight.

'It looked all over as Gaye Brief sailed past to the last, but, remarkably, it was not.

'Rallying gamely under Tony Mullins, Dawn Run fought back like a good 'un to give Richard Linley a momentary scare on the winner who had only a length to spare ...

'A tremendously impressive looking mare, built much more like a chaser than a hurdler, Dawn Run must be a Gold Cup prospect ...'

Dawn Run thrived in the spring air and, like many a sportsman or equine, also thrived on winning.

Many a grandstand critic considered that after her amazing Liverpool efforts, she should be turned away for her summer holiday. Paddy, however, lets his horses tell him what they want, and Dawn Run clearly showed that she was in peak form and condition on her return to Doninga. It therefore seemed quite justifiable to her astute trainer to run her two and a half weeks later in the BMW Champion Novice hurdle at Punchestown on 26 April. After all, this was a novice event, albeit a champion one, and it set the seal on the exciting season which had begun in very modest maiden fillies' hurdles.

'People tut-tutted about running her again, but she was really kicking and rarin' to go,' said Mrs Hill.

With such as Buck House and Mysterious Arthur, second and third to her in the Findus Beefburger, and good horses like Corrib Duke (second favourite) and Mrs Playfair (this time ridden by William Mullins) it was sure to be a good contest.

However Dawn Run simply galloped her rivals into the ground. She made every yard of the running, clearly revelling in her favourite occupation, and although Tony eased her on the run-in she still finished ten lengths clear of Mysterious Arthur. Corrib Duke was third and Buck House only fifth.

Now there was nothing left for Dawn Run but her summer at grass, and on 2 May she turned home to Waterford, to roam the Hills' thirty-three acres in the company of Dolly the hunter, Boro Nickel the brood mare, and co. She had won £35,924 in that first season's racing, beginning with that owner-ridden 'bumper'.

14

Which Jockey?

Dawn Run returned to Doninga on 18 August, sleek and well and the decision was made to keep her hurdling for another year with the Champion Hurdle now at the back of their minds. Should she disappoint, there was still time to switch her to chasing, the job for which she was bred.

First, Dawn Run had a 'warm-up' race on the flat to get fit, the two-mile Giolla Mear race at The Curragh on 22 October. Ridden by P. V. Gilson at 9 st. 11 lb, she was fourth, beaten by only a head for third place by Boreen Prince at 8 st. 10 lb, with the winner Ravaro and second, Liffey Locket both carrying only 7 st. 10 lb.

The race brought her on the proverbial ton, and when she went to Down Royal for the A. R. Ṣoudavar Memorial Trial hurdle she started at 5–2 on and trounced the opposition, yet again making all, and winning by her now customary ten lengths.

But in doing so, the mare had jumped badly left at the last, and young Tony Mullins had looked round for imaginary rivals several times. Could it be, now that the mare might really be going places, that the time had come to replace Tony by a more experienced jockey, one who would hold her together, especially at the last which was becoming something of a bogey with her?

Mrs Hill thought so, and broached the subject to her trainer who was, of course, the jockey's father, in time for the mare's next race, the two-and-a-half-mile Vat Watkins Grade 2 at Ascot on 18 November.

Opinions still vary widely in England and Ireland on the question of Dawn Run's jockey. There are those who say, justifiably, that the mare 'runs for Tony'. Equally, there are others appalled that a professional should ride her on such a long rein, giving the appearance of slackness.

Mrs Hill's mind was made up. In spite of the ease of the mare's Down Royal victory, she thought Tony had given her a 'terrible ride' there, and let her jump the last 'any old how'.

'I'm afraid of her getting into bad habits,' she said.

It was the first time she had been to Down Royal, and Dawn Run again showed her class. The Champion Hurdle was now beginning to look a distinct possibility. Naturally, she wanted the best possible jockey.

Mrs Hill said, 'When I told Paddy of my decision, he seemed almost relieved.'

It was November 1983, and Mrs Hill felt justified in asking for a change, and so it was, only three or four days before the Ascot event, that Paddy phoned Jonjo O'Neill to book him for the mare.

It is hard to imagine a more engaging, cheerful personality than Jonjo, with his ever-ready smile and sparkling bluey-green eyes. Born and brought up in Castletownroche, a village between Fermoy and Mallow deep in Co. Cork, his father, Tom, kept a grocer's store there and also dabbled in greyhound racing. Of his parents and three elder brothers, it was only Jonjo's father who had any slight interest in horses. Yet Jonjo cannot remember any time when he did not long to ride himself. Every school holiday the young Jonjo would visit the local farm to ride whatever was available; and competing in donkey derbies was one of his favourite occupations, not, perhaps, the most willing of nags on which to learn how to ride a finish.

Once he was about nine or ten and old enough to look after a pony himself, Jonjo's father bought him his first pony, Dolly, from the fair at nearby Tallow.

The dark bay mare with a white face was only sixteen months old, and cost Tom O'Neill the princely sum of £27 2s.

She stood about thirteen hands high which was really too big for the little lad, but he set about breaking her, helped by his father and a friend.

Dolly can be said to have paved the way for Jonjo's career. From the start, he looked on her as a stepping-stone towards the time when he could go into racing, an ambition fired by regular visits each spring to the area's point-to-points.

With her, too, he began following the Dunhallow hounds, a sporting pack whose ditches and fences are big and whose followers are fearless.

'Hunting fettled me up in every respect,' Jonjo recalls, and in this he is very like Mrs Hill (whose hunter is also called Dolly).

'It is the best training for a kid, doing lots of different things,' he says.

Jonjo still grasps any chance he can to hunt, usually with the Cumberland Farmers from his home at Skelton, near Penrith.

As soon as Jonjo was fifteen he left school and joined Don Reid, a small trainer at Mallow. After a year he transferred to Michael Connelly at Kildare, where he spent three years and finished his apprenticeship.

He rode out most days on the Curragh and, being very small, he had about seventy rides mostly on the flat.

Jonjo's first and only win on the flat in Ireland was in fact a half win, for he dead-heated on Lana in an apprentices' race on The Curragh on 9 September 1970.

He also had one win over hurdles for Mick Connelly at Downpatrick and one chase win at Navan.

But Jonjo found it hard to really get going in Ireland, partly because he found it a bit of a closed shop and partly because his boss, Mick Connelly, would usually sell any horse the moment it showed any ability.

Therefore, at the age of nineteen, Jonjo looked around for a job in England and, still very much at the start of his career, he joined Gordon Richards at Penrith in Cumbria.

Thus he left behind the beauties of his native Ireland for the splendours of England's Lake District, surely one of the

The Mullins family, left to right: Willie, George, Maureen, Paddy, Tony and Tom. Everyone of them has ridden a winner.

Dawn Run's first race. *Below:* her first win in June 1982 at Tralee. Her jockey: Ireland's Galloping Grandmother, Mrs Charmian Hill.

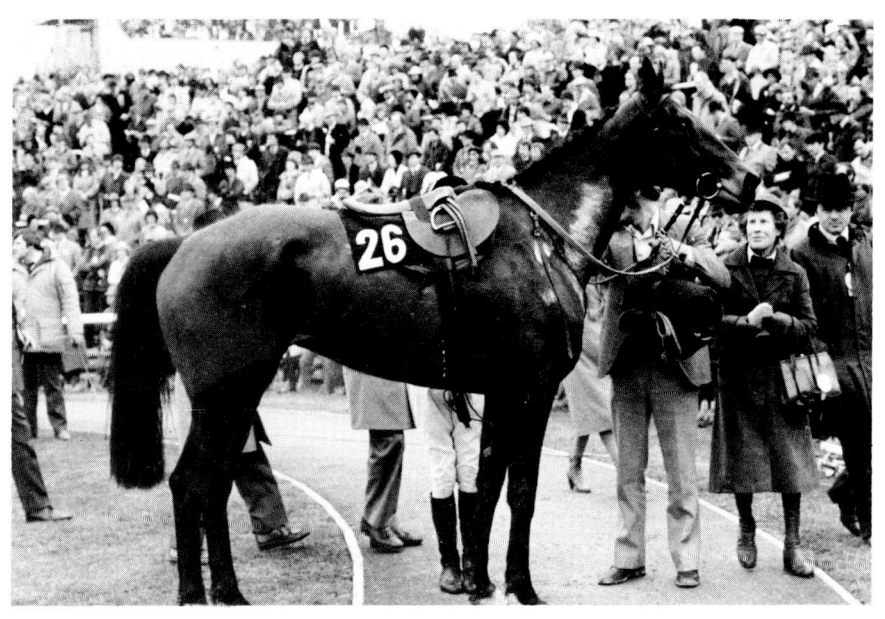

Dawn Run at Cheltenham in 1983. *Below:* three weeks later, Charmian and Oliver Hill receive the Sun Page Three Hurdle trophy at Aintree.

Jonjo O'Neill and Dawn Run coming over the last in the 1984 Cheltenham Champion Hurdle.

They are greeted by John Clarke, Dawn Run's lad and Jim Murphy, Paddy Mullins' travelling head lad. Cheltenham goes wild!

Dawn Run – well clear at the last in Paris.

A delighted Tony Mullins waves to the Paris crowd after Dawn Run had won the 1984 French Champion Hurdle. Dawn Run is led by Jim Murphy.

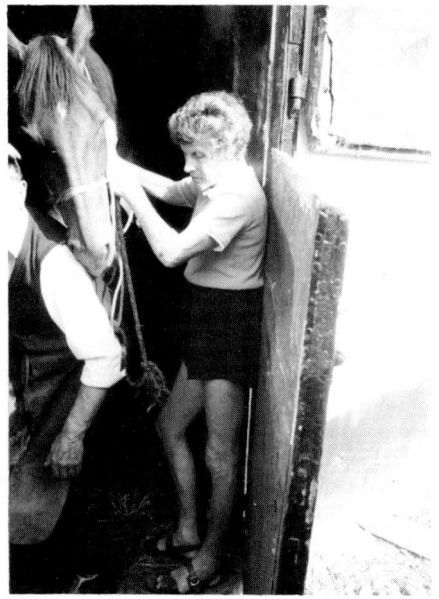

Opposite

Top: Charmian and Eddie Hill.

Bottom left: Dawn Run and friend at home.

Bottom right: The summer's rest is only disturbed by a visit from the blacksmith.

Above: An extraordinarily confident Tony Mullins takes Dawn Run down
to the start of her first race over fences ...

... and he was right! The mare
jumped beautifully and won easily.
Ireland hailed a new Arkle.

finest spots to choose for such a transition, and he began a sensationally successful five years with his new boss.

In no time at all, Jonjo was riding fifty to sixty winners a season and usually finishing in the top three in the National Hunt jockeys' table. But in 1977 he felt the time had come to make a break and go it alone.

It was a tremendous gamble to take. He was in one of the top jobs in the country, riding good winners and carving a fine reputation for himself. If he turned freelance and things did not go well, he would sink into oblivion in next to no time. Indeed, Jonjo did not even expect to do as well as he had with Richards. If he could ride say thirty winners a season he would be happy. That was the key word.

The decision and the year truly proved eventful. The season 1977–8 was that memorable one when he amassed 149 winners, only one short of the magical 150 and anyway a record. And to cap it, on 14 June 1978, two weeks after the end of the season and at the age of twenty-six, he married Sheila Mounsey, a pretty farmer's daughter.

Jonjo is now the proud father of three young children, Louise, Gillian and Tom. Only if they want to ride will he encourage them.

'I will let them carve their own careers in whatever sphere they choose and do my best to help.'

Skelton Wood End, his home, has forty-five acres, mostly accommodating young potential National Hunt horses, but with just enough sheep and cattle around to justify it being called a farm.

The phone call from Paddy Mullins a few days before Ascot offering the ride on Dawn Run came completely out of the blue. Naturally it was not the sort of ride one would turn down. Had Jonjo done so, it would only have been offered to someone else, rather than back to Tony Mullins. He knew the mare was 'fairly decent', having seen her run at Cheltenham and, especially, that second run at Liverpool.

In the event, the Ascot race nearly proved a disaster. The ground rode terribly firm. Paddy was in favour of pulling out. Mrs Hill stood firm; although, had it been in Ireland, she, too, would have withdrawn. But they had come to England, there were only six rivals and she looked to have their measure; to one of these, Amarach, she had given twelve pounds and a fifteen-length beating at Liverpool. Yet Amarach was now set to concede her five pounds mares' allowance. It should, as became customarily the case with Arkle in his heyday, be a piece of paid exercise.

The papers evidently thought so, too, and Eddie Hill borrowed a copy of one to help get his son and co-owner Oliver in. The Hills had only been given two tickets and there was none for Oliver and Vonny. Then he saw a headline that said Dawn Run should attract an otherwise thin crowd and he showed it to the gatemen. They still refused the tickets, until Eddie asked to see the Secretary.

The race was televized and in the preamble Dawn Run was hailed as Ireland's rising star. For many viewers it was not her ability that impressed, for she was far short of her best on the firm ground, failing to stride out as freely as usual, but her sheer guts.

When a front runner is passed by another horse near the end of a race, it is very, very rare for it to rally. Mares are not always the bravest, yet a good mare can be bravest of all, and one such is Dawn Run. Neither she nor Jonjo was happy as they led into Swinley Bottom. She was not jumping out on the firm ground, and it became a desperate race. At the last flight Dawn Run was headed by Amarach who went a length up and it looked all over. But incredibly it was not.

In what was probably the most uncomfortable race of her career, Dawn Run still refused to give up. Nine horses out of ten would have given up then. But Dawn Run, assisted by the strongest rider in the saddle, battled her great big heart out, forcing herself ever nearer. They passed the post locked together. But to most eyes the mare looked beaten.

Mrs Hill turned away, bitterly disappointed, certain they were defeated.

The public address announcement giving the photo verdict to Dawn Run by a short head came as the biggest surprise! The mare had won 'on the nod'.

Afterwards, Mrs Hill asserted, 'Amarach would never get within a million lengths of her again; it was only the hard ground, she wouldn't let herself go, but Jonjo taught her a lot.'

It had indeed been an epic struggle and one that had smashed the course record held since 1966 by a full four seconds. So it was no mean performance.

'Dawn Run Conjures Up A Record Show' was the *Sporting Life*'s headline above George Ennor's report of Dawn Run staging 'a thrilling fight back to snatch a record-breaking win'.

'Dawn Run Battles Home For Record' was the *Daily Telegraph*'s headline under which John Oaksey said, 'Dawn Run needed all her courage and most of Jonjo O'Neill's strength to scramble home ... she was clearly hating the ground, but still smashed Mayfair Bill's record by more than four seconds.' The victory was so narrow that many television punters telephoned the BBC to query the result.

John Oaksey added, 'This is obviously not a performance that will give Gaye Brief's trainer Mercy Rimell many sleepless nights – but equally clearly Dawn Run may well be a very different proposition on softer ground and a more testing course.'

Inevitably, after this close finish, the jockey question was raised again.

One Irish article, written just after Ascot, under the heading 'A Matter of Experience', read: 'Tony Mullins or Jonjo O'Neill? – the argument has raged all week. It does not relate to who is the better jockey – Mullins is still a novice in a field in which O'Neill has excelled for years – but rather who can get the best out of Dawn Run.'

Looking ahead, it was noted that the sad death of O'Neill's possible Champion Hurdle mount, Eckbalco, left Jonjo with no firm commitment for the build-up to the Champion Hurdle 'so the chances are his partnership with Dawn Run will be maintained. But Tony Mullins, anxiously waiting in the wings for any change of heart from the owner, has done little wrong on the Deep Run mare in the past.'

15

The Rivals

Having not had the best feel of Dawn Run at Ascot, Jonjo was not surprisingly still a little reticent about her prospects as a potential champion hurdler, but he flew to Ireland to team up with her again on 7 December in the Racehorse Trainers Association two-mile hurdle at Naas, and that made up his mind.

She and two others were set to carry 12 st. 3 lb; one was on 11 st. 3 lb and the remaining five all carried between 10 st. and 10 st. 9 lb. It was the first time she had had to carry so much weight and to make it more telling the ground was heavy.

She put in another gallant effort, leading until the last flight where, regrettably, she continued her trait of blundering, and Boreen Deas, a 33–1 outsider on 10 st. 9 lb, went on to score by three lengths. Potato Merchant never got in a blow to finish third.

Mrs Hill's first reaction was one of disappointment, but when she saw Jonjo's smiling face, she realized it was not too bad. A jubilant Jonjo declared in the unsaddling enclosure, 'This is champion material.'

The time had come for a full scale Champion Hurdle dress rehearsal, and the Ladbroke Christmas hurdle at Kempton Park on Boxing Day, where she was likely to meet Gaye Brief, was chosen for it.

Kempton is a very different proposition to Cheltenham. Where the premier course is undulating, wide open and testing, suited to a galloper who can stay: Kempton is flat and sharp, suited to a rapier's thrust of speed. The ground is light and drains quickly, unlike Cheltenham's which can quickly become heavy.

Gaye Brief was the reigning Champion Hurdler and suggestions that he could be seriously threatened by the Irish mare were scoffed at by his ardent supporters in spite of her proximity to him at Liverpool the previous spring. He had the class and the speed and the experience, but there were other observers who remembered that at Liverpool it was nevertheless the novice mare who had stolen the limelight.

A year older than Dawn Run, Gaye Brief is by Lucky Brief and is owned by Sheikh Ali Abu Khamsin whose support of National Hunt racing has been welcomed in recent years.

Christmas is not the easiest time for an Irish owner to come to England for a race, and this trip proved memorable for reasons other than the race itself for both Mrs Hill and Oliver.

The traditional Christmas lunch with all the hard work that that entails had been prepared and cooked by Charmian Hill for many of her family and enjoyed amongst much celebration. It is a time when most mothers, let alone grandmothers, gain a well-earned rest after it is all over.

Not so for Mrs Hill for Boxing Day – or St Steven's Day as it is known in Ireland – began for her in the early hours, leaving the house at 5.30 a.m. to drive to the airport. Dr Hill, on duty, stayed behind.

Oliver and Vonny made their own way having spent Christmas with Vonny's father in Belfast. They had had a 'ferocious party', and were feeling considerably the worse for wear when they boarded the plane. They had not been in the air long when a courteous steward remarked, 'You're not looking very well, sir. Would you like a drink?'

Before they knew it, they were drinking Bloody Marys. It was 11 a.m. By the time they caught a taxi to Kempton they were fairly inebriated, and on their arrival they made straight for the champagne and lobster bar.

Oliver laughs as he tells the story: 'First we thought we would drink some champagne before the race "in case she didn't win".'

As they were consuming lobsters and drinking champagne, they looked at the newspapers. All of them tipped Gaye Brief.

Suddenly Oliver looked at his watch. 'God, Vonny, the race is nearly on. Come on, quickly.' They jumped up from their chairs and ran out, pushing their way towards the paddock.

The horses were walking round the parade ring. The couple tried to charge in, but were confronted by four or five policemen each side of the entrance.

'You can't go in there,' one officer told them, 'it's not allowed.'

Oliver pulled himself up.

'I beg your pardon,' he said, 'how dare you say that to me, my horse is in there.'

'No, you can't go in there, the Queen Mother is there.'

'To hell with that,' said Oliver, 'my horse is in there,' and he dragged Vonny past them and into the paddock.

They found Jonjo standing on his own and went up to him, making small talk.

'Hi, there, Jonjo, nice to see you.'

'Oh.'

'Good trip down from Cumbria? Long old way, you must be tired?'

'Oh, no, not really.'

At this point Oliver realized he still hadn't seen the mare.

'She's late coming into the ring.'

Jonjo leant forward and said quietly, 'Er, guv, I think I'd better tell you – yours is in the next race!'

Oliver hadn't even noticed that Jonjo was wearing the wrong colours!

The ground was dry and fast, and all the indications were that it would suit Gaye Brief best. His trainer Mercy Rimell had put a pacemaker Migrator in the race and so for once, as Migrator set about his task, Dawn Run did not make all the running. Neither, thankfully, did she fight for her head and insist on taking on that horse, settling comfortably in Jonjo's hands until three flights from home when she cruised to the front, with Gaye Brief in close attendance. Then as *Time Form* put it so accurately, 'Gaye Brief discovered, as others had before him, that passing a top form Dawn Run after following her at a good pace for almost two miles is no easy matter. The harder Gaye Brief tried, the more Dawn Run seemed to be spurred on.'

First one and then the other showed just in front but in the end it was superior jumping which won the day – and that intangible quality, heart. Dawn Run relished the struggle, Gaye Brief maybe not quite so much. He may not have been too pleased to be challenged.

It was Dawn Run who jumped superbly and got away quickest from the last and by this time the crowd was roaring. It looked as though the Champion was going down.

But now Gaye Brief's speed came into play and as he set off up the run-in he was gaining ground all the way. But the post came just in time for Dawn Run and she held on by a neck. The unthinkable in the Gaye Brief camp had happened! Ra Nova and Janus, who finished third and fourth, were both 50–1.

Afterwards, Mrs Rimell made the somewhat surprising revelation that Gaye Brief had been held up in his work with a hairline crack in a cannon bone, and that he was in need of the race. But not a word of that had been mentioned beforehand.

The score between the two horses was now one all. The Champion Hurdle at Cheltenham in March should prove to be a thrilling decider. What a Christmas present!

Charmian Hill and Paddy Mullins couldn't spend too long celebrating as they had a plane to catch back to Ireland. They left the party given by the sponsors Ladbrokes to hail a taxi but there was none to be found outside the racecourse. So they trekked back to the party and found someone willing to give them a lift to Heathrow. Supper, as breakfast had been that morning, was eaten on the plane, then there was the long drive back to their homes.

Not surprisingly, it was an extremely tired Charmian Hill who walked up the small flight of steps to her home at about

10 p.m., more than ready for her bed after her exhausting, albeit elating day.

Eddie Hill, who had watched the race on television, was there to greet her.

'There's someone waiting in the dining-room to interview you,' he said.

'I couldn't possibly, I'm too tired,' was the understandable reply.

'They won't wait, go on,' he urged.

Reluctantly, she walked into the dining-room.

There to greet her, made by Eddie, was a life-size 'replica' of Jonjo, bolster body, turnip head, adorned by cap and goggles, wearing Dawn Run's colours, holding a whip – and a jeraboam of champagne. It was marvellous!

There were two and a half months until the National Hunt Festival, and Dawn Run was to have just one more race before it. It had been intended to run her in the Champion Hurdle trial at Haydock, where she was to meet her short head victim, Amarach, again, in January, but the meeting was abandoned because of snow. This may have been a blessing in disguise for Dawn Run. She had sailed over, but had had a bad crossing and it was the only time anyone can remember when she had not eaten up and neither would she stale. After that she always flew to her races abroad but sometimes returned by sea. So an alternative had to be found and on 18 February the mare was bound for Leopardstown, for the Listed Grade One Wessel Cable Irish Champion Hurdle.

It was only the second running of this race and until then the most important – and still the most famous and valuable – hurdle race in Ireland was the Irish Sweeps. Founded in 1969, this lost its champion equivalence when it became a handicap in 1976. It still attracts top hurdlers but invariably they have to give large lumps of weight away to inferior horses.

There were eight runners for the Irish Champion Hurdle. Dawn Run opened at 5–4 against but by the start was odds-on, 4–5, with Boreen Prince at 100–30 and Ra Nova 4–1 this time.

Never allowed to get too far ahead in Jonjo's capable hands, Dawn Run nevertheless was always at the head of affairs and jumped superbly.

To Charmian Hill's surprise Ra Nova 'took on' the mare, disputing the lead for half-way until he dropped back beaten. There was no serious threat in the last mile, Dawn Run responding to Jonjo's driving to beat Boreen Prince by five lengths.

It was a perfect 'prep' race for Cheltenham and although Gaye Brief was still an odds-on ante-post favourite for the Champion Hurdle, the British Press now started to pay far more attention to the Irish mare and to her remarkable owner who had, of course, been making Irish headlines in her own right for years past.

16

Meeting a Pair of Determined Ladies

Poor Paddy hates publicity but he endured the big race build-up now with grace and co-operation. Suddenly everyone wanted to know more about this Irish mare and her remarkable owner, and Maureen Mullins arranged several interviews for the British Press, including BBC Television.

A camera crew virtually took over Doninga for a day, headed by Richard Pitman who has become a polished racing reporter and television commentator since hanging up his racing boots.

The finished product was an excellent, lively, and well-informed film not only about Dawn Run but Charmian Hill, too.

It showed for fact what many may have otherwise taken for fiction. Here was a tiny grandmother galloping a huge mare, probably the best horse in Ireland, round and round the circular grass gallop at Doninga, leading the string and beginning to lap the tail-enders and, just when it really looked as if she might be being 'carted', pulling the mare up from the sound of her voice urging her to 'Whoa!' Paddy watched quietly, used now to this sight, and when pressed remarked, 'Well, sure, an' the mare enjoys herself.'

Mrs Hill also explains her position in the gallop: 'I'm always put in the front; well, if we started behind, the mare would pull me to the front anyway.'

After this glimpse of the Mullins' stable, the film crew

travelled down to the Hills' home in Waterford, taking over the study for re-take after re-take of the interview with Mrs Hill as the effusive Eddie, ever enjoying himself, 'directed' her.

'It was no good her saying she "hoped" our horse would win, or that it "might" win,' he explained, 'the public watching the film would want to hear her say, "she *will* win"', and that, indeed, is how the film ended.

The interview included, naturally, the controversial withdrawal of Mrs Hill's licence to ride and her annoyance over it clearly still showed; as did Eddie Hill's self-confessed relief. Mrs Hill also explained why she had liked Dawn Run at the Sales – 'because she walked like an athlete' – and described how close the bidding had come to her limit.

The gallops at Doninga were visited by Press as well as television, and the writers produced some lovely turns of phrase to capture the atmosphere and sense of achievement.

Jonathan Powell, described it thus: 'Dawn in County Kilkenny and a sixty-five-year-old grandmother of nine gallops past on Ireland's main challenger for the Champion Hurdle ...

'Together they complete five energetic laps of a tight circuit ahead of Paddy Mullins' string of horses.' He goes on to summarize the Charmian Hill/Dawn Run story – and she is still insisting, 'If they gave me back my licence I'd ride her over hurdles tomorrow.'

Powell examined the mare's Champion Hurdle prospects: 'Dawn Run, every bit as brave and determined as her owner, seems the only obvious danger at the moment to champion Gaye Brief in March. But already Mrs Hill is looking forwards twelve months further to the 1985 Cheltenham Gold Cup.'

It was becoming clearer daily, as form sorted itself out, that Dawn Run was the only apparent danger to Gaye Brief. Yet for Charmian, despite the exciting prospect, it was still not the real thing. Only one race really mattered in the National Hunt calendar for her, and that was the Cheltenham Gold Cup.

All the same, her steely nerves began to twitch a bit, and she had to live with Eddie's bubbling enthusiasm for everything that was happening to them. He was revelling in the publicity and the reflected glory.

'I own the owner and I train her!' he beamed exuberantly with a gleam in his eye. 'It's all such fun.'

And he was very, very proud of her and the part she had played in producing the horse that was now the talk of all Ireland and much of England.

He thrust a copy of Brough Scott's evocative *Sunday Times* article into the hands of any visitor, and read and re-read it himself:

'Sometimes in Ireland you are sure the leprechauns are laughing at you. Here was their champion racehorse thundering round a Kilkenny field on Wednesday morning with, astride it, not some thick-shouldered jockey-boy, but a little old lady so small and frail-looking that you want to keep the grandchildren off her at teatime.

'Dawn Run is the horse, whose twelve brilliant victories make her the spearhead of this month's annual Irish invasion of the Cheltenham Festival. Charmian Hill is the rider, at sixty-five some fifty-nine years senior to her mare, and with an approach to racehorse ownership about as far from the modern trend of 'quadruped as commodity counter' as trainer Paddy Mullins' easy-going country yard in Munster is from Aqueduct, New York.

'Not for Mrs Hill the vague weekly phone call or the distant view of the nag on the gallops. She not only bought Dawn Run herself, and completed the then three-year-old filly's early education, she was also in the saddle on a golden day in the summer of 1982 when Dawn Run sped away from a big field at Tralee for the first success of what has been one of the most meteoric climbs in Irish jumps.

'Sadly it was also Charmian Hill's final race-ride, for that very morning she had received a letter from the Irish racing authorities telling her she would be licensed no longer. "I think it was very unfair because I was riding better than ever," says this extraordinary little grandmother of nine without a trace of humour. "So I said to myself, 'Wow – this is one race we are going to win.'"

'More cautious souls might have thought it something of a wonder that Mrs Hill had a licence at all after surviving the terrible crash which had killed her horse Yes Man at Thurles two seasons earlier. Three months in hospital with crushed ribs and vertebrae, and with pins to keep her head atop the neck took thirty pounds off the old lady's already bird-like eight stone, and for ordinary mortals would have left an afternoon's knitting as the height of achievement.

'But even her family have long since stopped trying to fit the year's most unlikely sports person into any cosy mould. "Ah, we let her do her own thing," says her husband, Eddie, whose patients in Waterford were no doubt intrigued when the doctor's wife took to point-to-pointing at the ripe old age of forty-one, and then amazed as she continued to defy the years, moving on to bigger things when Irish racing allowed women to ride against men in 1973, finally bringing off a remarkable treble, winning on the flat, over hurdles and over fences (at the first attempt), all on the ill-fated Yes Man.

'Write this down enough times, and the fact that granny's galloping is now confined to hunting and early-morning training spins seems almost mundane stuff. Well, it didn't look too dull when Dawn Run was led out of the box last Wednesday morning. After all, this rangy, hard-faced mare is on the crest of the wave, making her a real threat to the Champion Hurdler, Gaye Brief, whom she has already beaten at Kempton. She's also no respecter of persons, being as good at striking out with her front legs as kicking with the back, and having a ruthless style of galloping best summed up by the legendary Irish orders: 'Jump off in front and keep improving your position.'

'Such horses are usually treated with a degree of awe in keeping with the weight of money Dawn Run will carry when Jonjo O'Neill heads her towards the first hurdle on Tuesday week. But Paddy Mullins hasn't saddled a thousand winners in such varied spots as Newmarket, Fairyhouse and Auteuil without developing the knack of turning special circumstances to his advantage. Now, as his wife and sons watched Mrs Hill gathering speed on consecutive laps of the large grass field outside the barn, he simply nodded with the wise satisfaction of a man who never uses ten words when one will do, and said: "The mare enjoys herself."

'When the Cheltenham battle honours are settled at the end of next week, with the usual lion's share for the Irish, many of us will shake our heads and wonder how they do it. If Dawn Run can draw Gaye Brief's trumps in the Champion Hurdle, some may even remember that Dr Hill's talents stretch to such things as sawing people in half at charity parties. "I've never done it to Charmian, but I have pulled her out of a few table-cloths," he said. "And I once got three people fainting in the front row when I sawed a boy's head off in Killarney."

'The Irish don't need magic to win at Cheltenham – they've got enough of it already.'

By this time the mare was working stronger and feeling fitter than at any time before. Not yet actually six, although officially so since New Year's Day when all thoroughbreds have their official birthday, she was still growing into full strength and Paddy Mullins, that wise, soft-spoken man, was becoming more and more confident that they would beat Gaye Brief in the Champion. The mare had improved by leaps and bounds since the last time the two had met, and even then the mare had come out best. It was not just fairy talk to think of winning. Her muscles bulged, her coat gleamed and she became more and more full of herself in the box, so that John Clarke had to avoid her playful nips or sideways kicks nimbly, and Charmian had to muster all her strength and mastery to hold her on the gallops.

Gaye Brief might be favourite, but there weren't many Irishmen who would hear of defeat for their mare!

Then only a week before Dawn Run flew to England came the astonishing news: Gaye Brief was out of the race! He had torn ligaments in his back and would not run again that season. Sadly it meant that the big clash would not now take place. The sportsmanship of Mrs Hill is such that she would most certainly have preferred to have Gaye Brief in the field.

The door for her mare now appeared wide open. Inevitably, she became the new favourite for the race, and money flooded on to her. It was said that secret tactics were to be employed. Previewing the Irish prospects for this 1984 Festival in *Horse and Hound*, Galtee More referred to Dawn Run as the glamour girl of the Irish raiders, but tradition is all against the mare in her bid for the Champion Hurdle as no mare has won the race since Keith Piggott triumphed on African Sister in 1939.

'The five pounds sex allowance,' he continued, 'may just tilt the scales in her favour.'

Dawn Run departed for England by air with her customary nonchalance, and as usual ate up well on arrival at Cheltenham racecourse stables. She was looked after and ridden by her usual lad, John Clarke, in her work inside the course.

Security was tight for leading big race contenders and no-hopers alike, and it was quite impossible for anyone without either trainer's or stable lad's pass to get past the gateman. He was just one of twenty-five stable guards who take turns around the country and who sit through the night in little more than a draughty hut, with a paraffin stove for heat and the *Sporting Life* for company, with a willingness, cheerfulness and complete integrity born with a sense of service to racing and very little more. Their pay has increased little over the years and bears no relation to the value of the horses they guard, and there is certainly no danger money for them.

They get to know everyone by sight and can 'sniff something irregular from fifty paces,' according to their Director of Security, Peter Smiles.

Racecourse Security Services keeps an ever vigilant eye on the sport and nowadays spends £1.7 million of Levy Board money (raised from betting) annually on maintaining and improving the security of British racing.

A major aspect of their work is the fight against doping and such enormous progress has been made in recent years that the job is mainly preventative. In 1984, for instance, 5,748 horses were routine tested and only six proved positive.

Diplomacy among security staff can take many forms, as

on the occasion at Cheltenham one National Hunt Festival when a priest arrived at the stables wanting to utter a benediction for Anaglogs Daughter.

The stable guard's duty allows no discretion and the priest was not allowed in. So the stable lad brought the mare out for the blessing. She lost her race by half a length.

There was no such pre-race ceremony for Dawn Run and as she ate up her bowl of oats on the morning of Tuesday, 13 March 1984, there was an aura of expectancy in the chill air.

Cheltenham would not be Cheltenham if it was not cold, but Charmian Hill had a different sort of shivers to contend with on the day. Wrapped up beneath her red coat (bought in a sale to wear with black trousers to represent her colours) she felt all of a dither, finding it far worse watching a race than riding in one. Many another owner (or mother of a jockey) will sympathize with her desire to be on her own to watch her horse; there is nothing worse than having to make small talk at such a time and even loved ones can find they are having their heads bitten off. So Charmian Hill walked away from the parade ring alone as the fourteen runners filed out to the course to canter past the stands to the two-mile start.

Dawn Run started at 4–5, and her nearest market rival was the novice, Desert Orchid, another front runner on whom many English hopes were pinned, at 7–1. He had impressed deeply on his six outings, with five wins and a second, and he too, looked well now. He had beaten Mercy Rimell's second string, the appropriately named Very Promising, 16–1 now, on his previous outing and it looked as if the sky could be the limit for him – *if* he could cope with Cheltenham's unique challenge. Of him, Mrs Hill says, 'He is the only horse I've seen jump as fast as Dawn Run.'

Also featuring in the betting were the 1982 Champion Hurdler For Auction and the horse that so nearly beat Dawn Run at Ascot, Amarach, both on 14–1. Cut A Dash, ridden by Johnny Francome for the successful Sussex lady trainer Nadine Smith, also looked well and was on 16–1 with Very

Promising and the Irish Boreen Prince whom Dawn Run had beaten in the Irish Champion Hurdle.

Not entirely out of the betting was Dawn Run's old rival Buck House, on 18–1, and he had had a nice confidence-giving win on his last outing. The complete outsider was The Foodbroker on 500–1, a Chilean-bred horse nicely turned out by jockey-turned-trainer Peter Haynes.

Back in Ireland at this moment Waterford was like a dead city. Factories were closed, classrooms emptied, and by strange coincidence most of those who were working just happened to take their tea-breaks at 3.30 p.m. and rushed to the nearest television sets. Horses and racing are very much a part of the Irish way of life, and they were proud of their representative across the water.

They were able to see Dawn Run full of spring and very bouncy down at the start as Richard Pitman described her to television viewers; Jonjo was relaxed, holding a loose rein, and chatting, a light pad under his saddle to prevent chafing the mare's sides. As always she did not wear a noseband; Mrs Hill's horses never do, because it can, if too tight, interfere with a horse's breathing.

Assistant starter Trevor Archer tightened the girths, his hunting crop knotted round his back, always with him in case a fractious horse should need extra encouragement to start; and always ready with a word of encouragement for the jockeys, too.

The roll-call made and saddlery checked, starter Captain Michael E. R. Sayers called the fourteen jockeys into line, many of them pulling down their goggles at the last moment for they can become steamed up if worn when only walking round. It is those minutes before the start of a race that can seem endless.

For Mrs Hill, having found her way to the Press Room to watch, it seemed interminable.

At spot on 3.30 p.m. they were off. Dawn Run was quickly into her stride and at the head of affairs. She disputed the lead into the first, then settled for Jonjo just in front without ever appearing to be doing things the hard way. Now the

113

'secret' tactics were plainly going to be the same tactics as usual.

The grey Desert Orchid, one of two runners for David Elsworth, had never before found another horse dictating the pace, and he managed to get into his customary lead as they galloped away from the stands and towards the hill, over the third flight. At the fourth Desert Orchid was half a length up, but then he was a spent force and dropped back.

It was a race in which Dawn Run threw off first one and then another challenger. With Desert Orchid out of the reckoning and three flights left as they reached the top of the hill ready for the downhill sweep, the pack bunched on Dawn Run's heels. It looked anybody's race. Former winner For Auction, ridden by Frank Berry, was there; so was another Irish horse Fredcoteri who had won the last two runnings of the Irish Sweeps hurdle; Cut A Dash was part of the pack, but he began to weaken, and so did Sula Bula. Very much in on the action was Very Promising.

Jonjo had Dawn Run on the inside, but there was little in it and as they levelled out for the second last the main challenger was her old rival Buck House.

The crowds held their breath. Charmian screwed up her hands, her chin jutted forward, her earnest eyes missed nothing.

As several of the bunch began to weaken, and Dawn Run and Buck House raced stride for stride in front, few noticed Jim Old's outsider Cima making a forward move in Peter Scudamore's hands. All eyes instead were on the Irish pair and as they jumped the penultimate Dawn Run received a hefty bump from Buck House; but it was Buck House who came off worse.

It would have been enough to put off many a lesser horse, but not Dawn Run. Now the race looked at her mercy as she headed for the final flight. But her regrettable trait of 'messing' the last continued and she landed completely flat-footed.

Jonjo picked her up with masterly horsemanship and set off up that last famous hill. But there was now a very real threat, for Cima had come with a superbly-timed run, jumped the last flight, and was gaining on the mare.

One thing Dawn Run does not like is to be beaten. As usual she would have none of it. She had seen off enough challenges; she would show this usurper also.

It looked desperately close to the roaring crowd, especially as she began to hang, too. Some thought she may have interfered, thankfully the camera patrol showed not. But Jonjo was never in any doubt about the result; he had more up his sleeve if needed. It was not; by three-quarters of a length Dawn Run won the Champion Hurdle, in record time. The stand erupted.

Very Promising lived up to his name (and was sold for a reported £75,000 after the race) finishing four lengths back in third, a length and a half ahead of Buck House. Fredcoteri was fifth, Cut A Dash sixth, Amarach seventh, Boreen Prince eighth, and former champion For Auction only ninth. Bringing up the rear were Robin Wonder, Desert Orchid, Sula Bula, The Foodbroker and, last of all, Fine Sun.

Even before these straggled over the line, Mrs Hill made a dash to greet her horse. But so did several thousand other people. As she ran down the steps from the Press Room at top speed, she tripped. Quick as lightning, a pressman shot out his hand and caught hold of her coat belt, saving her from falling in the nick of time, and she joined the stampede.

She managed to get to the walkway in time to reach hold of Dawn Run's reins and lead the mare triumphantly into the winner's enclosure, son Oliver, the part owner, at her side. Jonjo was leaning down shaking hands with all and sundry. Commenting on television, Peter O'Sullevan rightly pointed out that the owner, trainer, jockey and horse represented everything that was best in National Hunt racing.

'I have never seen such a reception or more popular winner since the days of Arkle,' he said.

Julian Wilson added the remark that Dr Hill had 'forborne with good humour the eccentricities of his sporting wife'.

As they walked into the enclosure the massive crowd erupted into cheering again, and mobbed the mare.

And that was only the start...

17

Better and Better

Never since Arkle had such scenes been witnessed. The Irish, almost to a man, burst into the hallowed winner's enclosure to hail their heroine. They nipped past the security men on the entrance, they climbed over the rails and under the netting. The end of the paddock reserved for the owners, trainers and riders of the first four horses only was flooded. Jonjo managed by only a hair's-breadth to hang on to the breastplate as souvenir hunters tried to take it.

To begin with Dawn Run took it as calmly as she does everything else, soothed by her devoted lad John Clarke, but even she began to fret at the tumultuous scenes that followed.

Mrs Hill was thumped vigorously on the back from all sides then her wildly enthusiastic supporters lifted her high into the air. She was clutching a bouquet of roses given by an Irish well-wisher who owns a fruit and flower shop and waved them happily to the crowd. As the red-coated, black-trousered grandmother was tossed and cheered, the chorus 'For She's a Jolly Good Fellow' rang out.

It says as much for the regard in which Mrs Hill is held in Ireland as for the mare herself that such a thing could happen and it was only when it was time for the presentations that things began to calm down. Any lingering doubt that the new enclosure was too impersonal was quelled for good.

'Don't they love it all,' said Captain Miles Gosling, the race-course Chairman. 'This is their hour and you can't blame them. And if I win the Champion Hurdle at her age, I'll go up in a balloon.' He then handed over to Waterford Crystal to make the presentations. Mrs Hill stepped forward to receive the huge trophy to more tumultuous cheers. For the first time since Waterford Crystal took over the sponsorship it was going home to Waterford. With the trophy went a complete set of Waterford Crystal and a cheque for £27,373, to the owner from winnings of £36,680, the difference going to trainer, jockey and stable.

Then Paddy Mullins stepped forward to receive the special trainer's prize of a Waterford Crystal trophy followed by Jonjo, smiling as ever, who was presented with more Waterford Crystal.

Jim Old sportingly congratulated the winners. His horse, Cima, had been plagued by problems since finishing second in the Triumph Hurdle of 1982. He had been hit by a lorry, rescued by firemen after two and a quarter hours, and given thirty-six stitches and then, when nursed back to fitness, went down with a virus, so he had no prep race for the Champion. He had run a blinder at 66–1.

Connections heard not a word from the trainer of the third, but several Press reporters quoted her next day as saying, 'Gaye Brief would have annihilated the opposition.' To do so, Gaye Brief would first have had to be in the line-up, which of course he was not.

Nine months later, when I met Mercy Rimell, she could not have been more full of praise for Dawn Run without a trace of 'mine's the best', although she did comment that Dawn Run was not necessarily the best hurdler. But her praise was wholesome: 'She's a great horse with tremendous courage, the best mare of all time and probably the best horse since Arkle.'

Jenny Pitman, who won the Gold Cup with Burrough Hill Lad two days after Dawn Run's Champion Hurdle triumph, also told me later in the year, 'If Dawn Run can win the Gold Cup then she's a champion the like of which has never been seen before, not in my lifetime, anyway.'

The crowd kept buzzing, unwilling to disperse. So much for 'secret' tactics. Dawn Run had run the only way she knew how, bravely from in front, and it would have been a mistake to try otherwise. It made the crowds admire her all the more and what everyone was talking about now was the prospect of the Champion Hurdle/Gold Cup double at long last becoming a reality.

It was probably the first time the question of the Gold Cup double had ever been bandied about at the time of a horse winning the Champion Hurdle. Such conjecture for Bula, Sea Pigeon and Night Nurse did not come about until after they had embarked upon their chasing careers.

It was a euphoric group which eventually walked back to the Cotswold Grange where they consumed one hundred bottles of champagne.

As for Dawn Run herself, she came home better than ever, in spite of her hard race; she just thrived on it. Soon she was voted Racehorse of the Year and Bravest Horse of the Year, both of which entailed gala visits to London later in the year for her intrepid owners (and Mrs Hill made herself a stylish outfit in silky black and red), as well as receiving many other accolades.

Nor was Dawn Run's season yet over. Eighteen days after her Cheltenham victory she flew to England again for the Sandeman Hurdle at Liverpool in which the previous year, when it was called The Templegate, she had astonished the racing world by running Gaye Brief to a length.

There were eight runners and no fewer than five of them were Irish. As in the previous year, the first three home in the Champion Hurdle were in the line-up, but this time there was no novice waiting in the wings to step out into the limelight. Dawn Run carried a penalty for her Champion win giving weight advantage to both Cima and Very Promising which, in theory at least, meant they should reverse the placings – but I don't think anyone really expected them to! Buck House, fourth in the Champion, was yet again facing the mare, and so were Fredcoteri, Mount Bolus and Daring Run from Ireland, and Permabos.

It was Grand National day (fifty minutes later Hello Dandy won the big race from Greasepaint and the 1983 victor, Corbiere) and this time Jonjo could not team up with Dawn Run.

He had accepted what could be considered a 'safe' ride on the grey Man Alive in the Topham Trophy on the Thursday, but had suffered a bad fall, causing his head to split open above his eye. This was stitched but he was forced out of the saddle.

So it was that Tony Mullins was back in the plate, and Dawn Run skipped round that course so merrily it was just as if she was out in an Irish Jaunting Cart, leading from start to finish with her ears pricked, jumping superbly, galloping in her own relentless rhythm.

Very Promising chased her in vain without making any impression and poor Cima, so gallant in the Champion, never got in any sort of blow, finishing right back in sixth.

It was a tasty *hors d'oeuvres* for the Grand National to follow, as Dawn Run skated home for yet another ten-length, mistake-at-the-last victory.

It re-opened two topics: should the mare stay hurdling instead of embarking upon steeplechasing next season? And, did the mare not run better for Tony Mullins?

Certainly Paddy Mullins was now entertaining thoughts of keeping the mare to hurdles, but Charmian Hill always insisted that chasing was to be her game, the hurdles successes a welcome bonus.

As for the rider, Tony Mullins had again looked round several times, something amateur Mrs Hill most certainly never did, but, although on a pretty loose rein, Tony did conjure a great run out of her – her leap at the third last flight was quite magnificent – and to some eyes it appeared that Dawn Run was a very different horse with Tony Mullins in the saddle.

The Liverpool race was probably her best performance of the season to date, whereas she had been involved in some pretty hard races under Jonjo. No one criticized Jonjo but several thought the mare, being a lady, simply ran better when she was allowed to do as she liked.

Charmian Hill thought otherwise. In her view Jonjo had taught the mare a great deal and that what is more, few other riders would have got her up to short head Amarach at Ascot, or into second place at Naas.

It was less than a year since, at Liverpool, Paddy was quoted as saying he did not think she had the speed for the Champion Hurdle and would go straight into chasing after her one season hurdling.

Yet when this incredible, meteoric second season was to end it was he who was in favour of a third season's hurdling while there were rich pickings for the taking. It was Mrs Hill who insisted on turning to chasing before her speed was blunted.

Paddy now thought that in view of the way Dawn Run slaughtered her field at Liverpool Mrs Hill might give serious thought to keeping the mare over the smaller obstacles for another season.

His mild voice barely containing his astonishment, he told anyone who asked, 'The mare just keeps getting better and better as the spring progresses and there is really no knowing just how good she really is.'

He announced that next on the agenda would be the French Champion Hurdle – and that could be the transition to chasing.

18

'Une Phénomène'

The remarkable improvement in Dawn Run continued when she returned home, so Mullins prepared her for the Prix La Barka, a two miles three and a half furlongs hurdle race at Auteuil, France's premier jumping track, at the end of May. This was a sensible step as one of the main reasons no English or Irish horse had ever won the French Champion Hurdle was because they could not adapt sufficiently to the strange Parisian obstacles.

But his decision met with plenty of criticism from 'pressroom trainers' who berated him for keeping her from her summer holiday. She had been running continuously since the previous September and deserved a break, they argued. She had the Champion Hurdle as well as all those other successes under her belt and the implication was one of greed that she should run again when, they also declared, the ground was sure to be hard.

As usual, instead of being able to shrug off or ignore bad press, as Mrs Hill could, Paddy was acutely sensitive to it, and Maureen loyally defensive.

Charmian Hill supported his decision fully. She knew he would only do what he considered best for her mare. It was now also understood that, with Tony having regained the ride at Liverpool following Jonjo's injury, he would partner her again in France.

Her exercise at home was, as usual, shared between her lad John Clarke and Charmian Hill who visited as often as possible. Mrs Hill also accepted an invitation to parade Dawn

Run at Punchestown, the sole remaining Irish track with some races over banks and a meeting that is full of atmosphere. Its magnificent view stretches into the far hills and granite rock outcrops almost abut the far side of the course.

The pair were meant to just walk and trot round but, to the consternation of not a few onlookers, Mrs Hill allowed the world's most powerful hurdler to go on at such a lick down the middle of the course that they thought the aged grandmother was being run away with.

'But,' she explained afterwards, 'sure, an' she doesn't show herself off properly at the slower paces. I wanted them to *see* her!'

She added, 'She's got a lovely temperament, really lovely. She'll take a fierce hold but she'll never do you down; she'll always go where you tell her and no matter how fresh she is I can always pull her up. If I have to, I can, she never goes mad. Ah, she's gorgeous!'

No harm was done by the episode and at the end of May she flew to France fit and well and ready to face the strange new obstacles. And strange they were, too, more like mini steeplechase fences than the traditional hurdles of Irish or English tracks, but upright, not sloped, so that they could be jumped from either direction, each with a two-foot ditch and guard-rail on one side like a miniature open ditch. Made of birch, they stood 3 ft 8 in high and were almost 4 ft wide. No wonder no visiting challenger had ever beaten the French in their own Champion Hurdle. This was a different ball-game altogether.

Mrs Hill and Oliver met Paddy and Tony after they had walked the course and they looked at the huge, verdant sward accommodating three separate courses sweeping past the luxurious grandstand. None voiced their fears but their unspoken thoughts were to wonder if this time they had bitten off more than they could chew. Could the gallant mare really adapt to a course like this? At least the ground was in her favour, for it had been watered so well that it was actually soft. So much for those know-it-all journalists, but they would still be quick to condemn should the visit prove a failure.

The course was wide enough to take a field of up to thirty runners comfortably and as they walked back to the buildings they learnt that most of the horses were trained around Paris, only about one-fifth out in the provinces. Most meetings are centralized, too, although some 170 tracks are dotted around the country, many used just once in conjunction with a festival.

They barely saw the early races, some of which had half-breds and even Anglo-Arabs running in them, for all their minds were concentrated on preparing Dawn Run. There were ten runners including the useful World Citizen.

Charmian Hill, clutching her bag nervously, reached the stands just in time to witness a curious French custom, that of jumping a practice fence down by the start. Dawn Run took it as if it were the most normal thing in the world and some confidence returned to the worried watchers.

Only a few minutes later she answered all their fears in no uncertain manner. She revelled in the new experience and illustrated that her exceptional adaptability was one more integral part of her multi-faceted make-up.

Her lead looked invincible but then she took off so early at one of the ditches – 'a million miles away' in Mrs Hill's words – that she landed with one leg in the ditch on the far side. They held their breaths for she would surely fall. It was amazing that she did not, but it did check her and the other runners closed the gap.

Oliver gasped, 'Oh, she's tiring.' But then she pulled away again.

Only the favourite World Citizen, to whom, like all the others, she was conceding a *stone*, made any sort of challenge in the home straight, but Dawn Run never saw him, or any other horse throughout the race for that matter, and, having learnt her lesson, jumped the remaining 'flights' faultlessly.

She scored by an official margin of one and a half lengths, although it looked more like six to many eyes, to widespread acclaim. The result printed in the Racing Calendar had only two words of comment printed beside Dawn Run: Made all. The little French experiment had turned into a dress rehearsal serving as a warning to the French of what they could expect in their own Champion Hurdle in three weeks' time.

And after the race Paddy said Dawn Run was *still* improving.

They were congratulated by M. Alan de Breil, president of the pristine course which during that long, hot summer of 1984, when surrounding land was indeed baked out, was lush and green, the covering grass thick and long.

He told them of his past attempts at luring English and Irish challengers, wining and dining several trainers but after they had walked the course they had all declined to send any horses.

'Steeplechasing lacks international confrontation,' he said, 'but there is such a big difference in the courses that where the French horses learn to brush through, the English and Irish come a cropper. This is where your horse is absolutely exceptional.'

A few had made attempts on the French Champion Hurdle, like Gaye Chance and For Auction, and the French Grand National, too, like Tied Cottage and Spartan Missile, but none had won the hurdle and only Mandarin, back in 1962 – that memorable occasion when a broken bit dangled from his mouth and a weakened-from-wasting Fred Winter was in his saddle – brought about a fairytale win by a head.

It was not long before M. de Breil was welcoming the Irish contingent back again, this time with many more followers. It was 22 June and Auteuil sparkled like a green oasis surrounded by endless Parisian suburbs under the bright summer sun.

A breeze kept the midsummer day comfortably cool. It was the time of year when all English jumpers and the majority of respectable Irish ones were enjoying their summer holidays, grazing and ambling contentedly through their paddocks, the rigours of the winter sport behind them, thoughts of future ones not yet entertained.

Gradually the crowds trickled in to the smart suburban course close by the Bois de Boulogne, turning in off the A12 only a few miles from the centre of Paris, or walking through the long subway under the course from the Metro to the main enclosure.

The sight of a Dublin duty-free plastic carrier bag swinging incongruously from the arm of an Irishman was the only hint that today, perhaps, could bring something special.

A group of compatriots, clutching bundles of unfamiliar French francs, made their way to the Pari Mutuel, the equivalent of our Tote, while outside the horses were prepared for the day's feature race, the *Grande Course De Haies D'Auteuil* – the French Champion Hurdle.

One hundred, two hundred, five hundred, even a thousand pounds worth of French francs were placed on number four, the Irish mare. She could not be beaten, of this the rash Irishmen were sure. Never mind that no English or Irish horse had ever won this race before despite several attempts by the best. Never mind that she was of the weaker sex; or that she looked like an ungainly commoner besides the classily-bred little French *pur-sang*; or that she had never before raced beyond a distance of two miles and five furlongs and this was three miles and one and a half furlongs; and never mind that the winner for the last two years was again in the field bidding for a hat-trick. The mare was different. Sure, an' she would prove it. . . .

Charmian Hill was not to be seen near the Pari Mutuel; the biggest bet she had ever placed in her life was still ten pounds. For her, the *fun* was the thing. She lent over the rail of the pre-parade ring with Eddie and Oliver waiting for Paddy to arrive with the saddle.

Back in Co. Cork, Dawn Run's breeder John Riordan wondered what was happening in Auteuil and recalled those days of her illness as a foal. How close she had been to death, how bravely she had won her battle for life. Little could he have known then that that would become her trade-mark; and here she was, bidding for a unique international champion hurdle treble.

Now she had another battle on. As Dawn Run walked serenely round the pre-parade ring rumours were rife that she was going to be 'done'. The French were going to 'murder' her. One trainer had put three horses in the race one of which, a complete no-hoper ridden by the toughest girl jockey that side of the Channel, was, it was said, going to cut her off early in the race.

Charmian talked anxiously to English journalists Brough Scott and John Oaksey, her determined chin thrust slightly forward, her eyes darting about concernedly. There was nothing they could do, the mare must simply take her chance. Lax security did little to instil confidence. Anyone, it seemed, could walk into the pre-parade area. It would not be hard to 'nobble' her.

The parade ring itself was just as slack. Horses only came into it for mounting, it being more ornamental than practical with a concrete path weaving a figure of eight round the bushes and shrubs. French racegoers do not have a long, hard look at runners before a race; they assess their chance more on the form book than on what they look like, and visiting the Pari Mutuel is their chief pre-race preoccupation. But if an unauthorized person wanted to wander into the paddock there was little to stop him.

Sitting in the weighing-room, *'les Balances'*, trainer Paddy Mullins waited motionlessly for Tony to emerge from the changing-room. The quiet man of Irish racing, he is the epitome of a master at his craft. Never one to talk much, his eyes missed nothing from beneath his slanting Panama hat. Maureen, in a pretty dress to suit the sun and the occasion, her fair hair reaching down nearly to her shoulders from beneath her smart large-brimmed hat, sat quietly at his side with a ready smile.

'This is the worst part,' Paddy murmured quietly. 'Normally my job, the training, is over by now, but not when your son is riding.'

At only twenty-two years old, Tony's task could have weighed heavily on his shoulders, but he possessed the exuberance of youth, an optimism not yet dulled by too many falls or failures. He emerged from the changing-room, his bright, eager, sharp-featured young face sporting the red jersey with black hoops that were becoming so famous.

It was the previous dual winner World Citizen which opened as favourite. Victor over England's Gaye Chance in 1982 and over the Irish winner of the Champion Hurdle For Auction a year later, he was a bay seven-year-old by Great Nephew, owned, like Video Tape in the same race, by Daniel Wildenstein.

Lean and classy in comparison to the Irish challenger, he looked the part. The odds indicated the mare at a generous 7–2 or 3–1 but it is only the starting price which counts on the Pari Mutuel system and soon the weight of Irish-owned money brought her price down until she started at 6–5 favourite.

The big bay mare walked round nonchalantly, her ears half cocked, her small star showing white between her dark, honest, wide-set eyes, oblivious to the money at stake on her, unaware of the possible dangers lurking ahead.

The mare wasted little nervous energy in the preliminaries, saving all her strength for when it was needed most, in a race. This race was at level weights so that truly the best should win.

The signal for the jockeys to mount was given. The female jockey at the centre of the 'murder' intrigue stood tall and slim, resting one leg, her arms folded across her orange, blue and grey colours, her long fair hair tied in a pony-tail and falling down her back. Her horse, appropriately, was called Brouhaha, and at eleven years old it was clear he was not in it to win. ...

Dawn Run's lad for the day, Jim Murphy, swung her head inwards to face the centre of the paddock. Paddy Mullins checked the girths once more, tightened the surcingle, uncrossed the stirrup leathers so that they fell into place each side of her big, well-proportioned body, then deftly legged his son up into the saddle and as she paraded out of sight walked away, his head slightly inclined as was his custom.

The ten runners lined up. Dawn Run was in the centre of the well-watered course. Tony Mullins had walked it twice and knew which patches to avoid for the going had been made heavy in places by the efficient watering system; without it, the course would have been bone-hard and parched.

To the horror of the clutch of English and Irish watchers, Brouhaha lined up beside the mare, too late for Tony to do anything about it and, as the tapes went up, it looked for one awful moment as if she was set on a collision course.

Within seconds any would-be threat was over. Any intention to chop her up on the first bend was gone beyond recall as the mare went straight into a commanding lead.

To be fair, there most certainly never was any malicious intent and Brouhaha's rider is, I am assured, a 'charming little girl and a very sweet person incapable of such villainy'. Brouhaha was a proven stayer and with prize money going down to fifth place, he was there with some sort of chance of collecting a prize.

Even by the time they reached the first flight Dawn Run was more than five lengths clear, and she scorched round the first bend out on her own. By the fourth of the sixteeen flights she had the field toiling in her wake, strung out behind her more like hunters than France's top hurdlers.

But was she *too* far in front? Would she expend her energy and fall back beaten prematurely? After all, she was being tested over the furthest distance she had yet faced, and was hardly conserving her energy.

But she was just toying with them in her own inimitable catch-me-if-you-can style. Going out into the country for the last time she was an incredible fifteen lengths clear, with the best part of the long final circuit still to come.

World Citizen and Video Tape tried to challenge. They fell away beaten without getting in a blow. Dawn Run met two of the last four flights wrong. Tony let her 'fiddle' them. The spectators drew breath. Was she yet going to be beaten? It looked as if she could be tiring and her lead was halved.

Tony Mullins, sensibly, however, was only giving her a breather, and still she was eight lengths ahead as he steered her wide, very wide, round the last bend to avoid the wet. There were just two more fences and that long, long run-in to come.

They closed on her a bit, but it was only second fiddlers' play. She never saw them and won in a canter, pulling up.

The Parisians hailed this heroine, the best they had ever seen, with rapturous applause, throwing off all inhibitions to cheer her triumph warmly.

Officially Mister Jack was six lengths behind her, with Salute third and World Citizen and Video Tape a burnt-out fourth and fifth. No wonder they had been carried off their legs. The time for the distance was just six minutes and two seconds. It was a devastating, world-beating performance.

It was two years exactly since that first humble win in a bumpers' event at Tralee. Then it had been her veteran owner/rider from Waterford Mrs Charmian Hill who had stolen the headlines, having that very morning heard that her licence would not be renewed on grounds of her age.

Now it was the mare's turn as she stormed away with the third leg, worth more than forty thousand pounds, of a unique champion hurdling treble; the mare with the heart of a lion, the will-power of a tigress, and the nature of a lamb who had captured the hearts of racing folk. *Une Phénomène.*

19

In Arkle's Footsteps

Dawn Run spent the remainder of the summer wandering at will around the Waterford acres of Belmont in the company of Dolly the hunter, Boro Nickel the brood mare who had played such an important part in Mrs Hill's early point-to-pointing successes, a foal and a yearling, making five serene bay ladies nodding their heads contentedly, not a care in the world.

Neither did all the success turn the Hills' heads. Trophies were placed discreetly around the house, racing photographs displayed mostly in the sunny little study. The tall Champion Hurdle trophy itself stood on top of a corner table and was usually filled with flowers from the garden.

The couple's new-found wealth did not change their way of life. In her first two years of racing, Dawn Run earned just short of £200,000, a staggering tax-free sum by National Hunt standards, less all the various percentage reductions. Sure, there were *little* ways in which things altered. When the old washing-machine packed up, for instance, they did not have to think twice about ordering a new one; and for their 1984 Christmas trip to Australia they flew first class for the first time. But when it came to doing up the antiquated bathroom they had second thoughts. The deep, old-fashioned bath was so *comfortable*. Perhaps they could simply get it re-enamelled. . . . One investment they made as a direct memento of Dawn Run was to commission Jean Walwyn to sculpt a bronze of the mare.

Also in 1984 the brood mare Boro Nickel visited Deep Run.

'I could never afford him before!' expostulated Mrs Hill, throwing her hands up in horror. 'Then I saw an advertisement for him using a picture of Oliver and me leading in Dawn Run after the Champion Hurdle – I thought perhaps they owed me a nomination for that.'

After nine weeks at grass Dawn Run returned to Doninga in September and Paddy was delighted with her condition, preferring his horses not to come in too fat from grass.

John Clarke took care of her again and, amazingly, it was discovered that she had grown an inch since the previous autumn, between five and six years, and she now stood 16.3¼ hh, exceptionally tall for a mare. She had also acquired a splint on the inside of a foreleg, a bony growth which thankfully was away from the tendon and not likely to cause any trouble.

Mrs Hill was adamant that Dawn Run should now go chasing and although not a universally popular decision Paddy concurred and set about schooling her in a thorough and professional manner. Both owner and trainer agreed that, should the venture prove a failure, she could revert to hurdling.

Summer remained long into the autumn of 1984, making the ground so hard that Paddy could not run his best horses. It meant Dawn Run missed her normal 'warm-up' race on the flat and delayed some of her schooling.

When she did first go to The Curragh for her initial session the ground was slippery and the schooling was quickly halted rather than risk anything going wrong at such an early, crucial stage. But after that, in the hands of both Tony and William Mullins, she schooled after racing at Limerick Junction and Dundalk, both of which had the benefit of a raceday atmosphere and full size fences. She was a natural. But now the time for the real test had come. . . .

The Nobber Chase at Navan was one of a new autumn series of four novice chases leading up to a final at the Leopardstown Christmas meeting. It might have been designed especially for Dawn Run. It was worth a healthy five thousand pounds to the winner (peanuts, of course, to the fifty thousand pounds earned in her last run in Auteuil) and a twenty-four thousand pound bonus lay in store for any horse which could win two of the four *and* the eight thousand pounds final.

Dawn Run had already missed the first one because of the ground, and that had been won impressively by her old rival Buck House. So he had made the transition from hurdling to fencing smoothly and, to add piquancy and a useful yardstick to the contest, he was lined up against her now.

Navan lies about twenty miles north-west of Dublin in windswept Co. Meath. Dr Hill took the wheel for most of the long journey from Waterford until to her relief, Mrs Hill took over at Naas. By concentrating on the drive there was less opportunity to worry about the race. There were, after all, plenty of people who would be quick to say Dawn Run should have stayed hurdling should her venture into chasing prove a flop. They would conveniently forget that she had shown how adaptable and versatile she was when in France.

The morning that began dull and wet only got worse. By the time Eddie and Charmian Hill reached Co. Meath the rain was lashing down. The beech trees lining the road glimmered yellow and gold and russet through the murk and ivy clung to dead elms. There were several studs and biggish farms in an area evidently wealthier than the far south but not of the order of Ireland's green central plain. Visibility was atrocious and huge puddles appeared on both sides of the winding roads, fallen leaves floating on them. Could it even be that the course would become waterlogged and the meeting abandoned?

'We've had such a long dry spell the course can take it,' Paddy Mullins asserted.

For Mrs Hill it was a case of the more rain the better. 'There can't be too much for us,' she said.

The race was only two miles, but Navan was the undulating course which had originally been chosen to test Dawn Run's stamina as a hurdler and that, combined with the mud, would be to her advantage now.

Driving into Navan, a town marred by its tall television

aerials, messy factories and a dog track on its outskirts, the rain was coming down in torrents, but nothing was going to deter the Irish from coming to see their champion and they rolled in. There were no signs to the races, not even a sign into the course itself!

In front of the stands the beautiful view of the course opened up. It was a large, undulating, long oval track with low, tree-studded hills spreading into the distance beyond. The tiny members' lawn was partitioned from the rest of the public area by a fish pond.

The Nobber Chase was third on the card. The rain eased off, almost to the point of clearing up, or maybe it just wasn't noticed for that race, for it was certainly pouring down again later.

A group of spectators, mackintosh collars turned up, lined the path outside the stables down which Dawn Run was about to walk to the paddock, a touch that was reminiscent of the days of Arkle.

Dawn Run fidgeted as her surcingle was tightened, and a piece of velcro flapped loosely off one of her protective boots. She looked around her in that same imperious, interested, way that Arkle used to himself.

Those who had waited round the paddock caught only a fleeting glimpse of their heroine, for most of the runners were already mounted, and she did not hang about for long in the wet. Within a few minutes she was squelching her way down to the start along the funnel beside the finishing straight, past the stands to what would be the second last fence after a circuit, a buoyant Tony Mullins once again perched in the saddle.

She had opened at a generous evens, thanks to the presence of Buck House and her as yet unproved chasing ability, with Buck House a shade odds-on, but her fans were not to be insulted. By the off she was 4–5 on, and Buck House 7–4 against; of the remaining seven only the grey Dark Ivy featured in the betting at all.

As so often, events proved the bookmakers right. There only ever were the three horses in the race. No, that's wrong. There was only ever *one* horse in the race, with two playing a supporting role, a deferential distance behind. The rest were nowhere.

Dawn Run had created a pattern of setting up long leads in her hurdle races with Tony Mullins, but to do so in a chase might be fraught with danger. There is a big difference between 'fiddling' a hurdle at full speed and a big, black, stiff birch fence.

But the mare's brilliant performance on her chasing debut was a privilege to witness. It was a supremely and typically sporting gesture of her owner to send her chasing when big prize money in the 'safer' hurdling field was at her mercy.

The tapes flew up and Dawn Run showed straight away in the lead but sensibly Tony Mullins did not let her go out way in front. Neither was she pulling. She just lobbed along, completely at ease and so obviously enjoying the new experience. Life for Dawn Run was *fun*.

Tony rode her on a nice length of rein. She pricked her ears and lifted off magnificently at the first fence, just slightly pitching on landing. There was a slight drop there, and Tony said afterwards that she landed in a hole.

The great mare strode uphill towards the second, which would be the last fence next time round, and flew over it beautifully like a veteran to the applause of the crowd. She came squelching past the grandstands on the long run to the third. This was the open ditch, or 'regulation' set on the sweeping left-handed bend. Once more she pricked her ears, took a good look, and powered forward, attacking it like a lion pouncing on its prey, measuring her stride perfectly. Already this was an exhilarating display. She was three lengths ahead of Buck House, but Tommy Carmody moved that horse up to within a length as they approached the fourth. This was the first in the back straight and slightly downhill. It was the one which had caused her connections most fear beforehand, and now she was being bustled by Buck House, too. But the lady was not for hustling.

The fifth fence, at half-way, was probably the most significant of the race because Dawn Run met it all wrong. This is when a novice, or a big horse (and Dawn Run was both) could go headlong into it and somersault or, at best, make such a blunder that it would be stopped in its tracks.

Not a bit of it! Dawn Run not only has ability, power and size but the agility of a big cat and superior intelligence. Big she might be, cumbersome she is not. She put herself right so succinctly that it was barely visible from the stands on the far side.

'She sort of side-stepped,' Tony said afterwards.

Whatever it was, she actually *gained* two lengths in mid-air. Defeat began to look out of the question, but Buck House and Dark Ivy, by now ten lengths clear of the rest of the field but not far behind Dawn Run's heels, were keeping up their task manfully.

Going into the sixth of the ten fences, Buck House was still closing, but not once in the race did any horse make ground on Dawn Run at an obstacle, and she sailed majestically over that one. One of the things that made Arkle so great was his fantastic jumping. He went to England in November 1962 for his first chase, the Honeybourne at Cheltenham, scene of his three great Gold Cup triumphs. It is easy to forget just how brilliant he was, and sometimes comparisons are made prematurely when a new chasing star emerges. Dawn Run has a long way to go of course to match his record (a staggering twenty-two chase wins from twenty-six runs) but she has a far superior hurdling record (thirteen wins from nineteen runs, including three countries' championships, to Arkle's four wins from just six runs), and her claim is far superior to many other rashly made ones.

Jumping is the name of the chasing game and without the consistent ability to cross thick birch fences economically and safely, even flamboyantly at speed, a steeplechaser, no matter how good, will never be great.

Now as Dawn Run approached the last fence on the far side, four from home, Buck House was still on her heels but Dark Ivy had dropped back. The rest were effectively out of it. Tony had Dawn Run on the inside and as she flicked over it and wheeled gracefully into the bottom long curve towards the final 'regulation' three from home, Buck House was two lengths back. From there Dawn Run came away like a good 'un; her superiority and sheer class saw her lengthen that great stride towards the last two fences and home.

Approaching the last fence her two principal rivals were hard at work, their jockeys scrubbing and pushing, their good horses looking very ordinary indeed as Dawn Run galloped further and further ahead. As she skipped over the last, giving it inches of daylight, her long, curved ears pricked as ever, Buck House toiled in her wake, so tired that he virtually climbed over and Dark Ivy went by him.

The big bay mare was lolloping up the run-in. Long before she reached the line, with Tony easing her, the crowds in the stands literally erupted. The ovation could probably he heard in Navan town!

This was no grey, wet day for the Irish, but possibly the most exciting they had had on a home racecourse for twenty years. They were witnessing a phenomenal mare. There were a good many wet eyes as well as hoarse throats as the red and black colours passed the post and a *stampede* followed towards the winner's enclosure. Normally sedate people ran as hard as, but with less effect than, their heroine had just done! This is what jumping is all about, enthusiasm, sportsmanship, heroes and heroines. Big business is not for this sport!

The crowd thronged round, all eyes on Dawn Run. The second and third might just as well not have been there. All nine runners completed the course, some of them *two fences* behind the winner!

Mrs Hill's bright, shining eyes darted about as she answered a barrage of press questions amid the general euphoria. Paddy looked pleased and much more relaxed; Tony was elated; Dr Hill was in his usual vintage form; and Oliver and Vonny smiled happily.

Both Mrs Hill's and Paddy Mullins' initial reaction was the same: relief that it was over. Had Dawn Run failed they would have been on a hiding to nothing. Mrs Hill's decision (endorsed by Jonjo and many others) to switch to chasing a full year sooner than many other people considered necessary, had been fully vindicated.

'Now bring us back the Gold Cup,' called out one of the spectators crushing against the railings. Everywhere there was excitement.

Mrs Hill, her voice rising and falling excitedly, exclaimed, 'She's so clever, she can change her feet in two seconds; she's unbelievable.'

'It looked as if she'd been chasing all her life,' echoed a beaming Dr Hill.

'Don't forget to weigh in,' shouted a spectator to Tony.

Immediately after the race one firm of bookmakers quoted Dawn Run an incredible 4–1 joint favourite for the 1985 Gold Cup with the holder Burrough Hill Lad. Another bookmaker put her 6–1 second favourite to that horse. But even as Dawn Run was still cooling off in the winner's enclosure, Paddy Mullins told the eager Press men, 'No, not the Gold Cup this season, the Sun Alliance Champion Novice Chase – the Gold Cup for 1986.'

The wise man was not going to be hustled into hasty decisions. The mare was worth waiting with. Captain Christy was the last horse to win the Gold Cup in his first season's chasing (and coincidentally his winning debut had also been on 1 November) but after his famous victory at seven he had not really carried on.

Mill House won it at six, but that was when Arkle went for the same novice chase that was intended for Dawn Run (then called The Broadway), before beating Mill House the following year at the start of his Gold Cup hat-trick. Patience is another integral part of the jumping game. So the plan was for Dawn Run to run in another qualifier, then the final at the Leopardstown Christmas meeting, keeping her at home in Ireland for the first half of the season.

Comparisons between champions of different eras can be odious, and with prize money earnings pointless because of inflation. Nevertheless, this victory justified Dawn Run's comparison with Arkle; and it took her prize-money winnings to over £200,000. And it couldn't happen to nicer, more genuine people. All over Ireland, I have never heard anything but wholesale praise and admiration for Charmian Hill.

The Press was ecstatic. 'Dawn Run has World of Chasing at her Feet', headed Michael O'Farrell's report in the *Irish Times*.

'Dawn Run's Super Run', was the *Irish Press* headline above Tony Power's glowing article, and 'Echoes of Arkle in Dawn Run Victory', was the *Daily Telegraph* headline.

John Oaksey, that paper's reporter (as Marlborough) also had a full page in the following week's issue of *Horse and Hound* devoted to the mare under the heading 'Dawn Run Fills Damp Air with Golden Dreams'.

For Michael O'Farrell it was 'a privilege to see Dawn Run perform so brilliantly on her first appearance over fences'. When pressed by Buck House, she 'Arkle-like, just went away. Each stag-like jump brought a gasp of admiration from the large crowd who braved the weather to see her run.'

Tony Power, describing Dawn Run's 'spectacular transition' from hurdling to chasing, declared that the winner of the English, Irish and French Champion Hurdles 'must be the most exciting National Hunt horse in training since the balmy days when Arkle bestrode the world of jumping'.

He praised Paddy Mullins' training as a 'classic example of a jumper produced perfectly to do the job,' adding, 'the mare's attitude to the race was remarkable in a debutante. She measured her fences, picked her strides and take off point, and when she got a bit close to the first fence down the back straight, she had the brains to stick in a short one and jump the fence perfectly.'

John Oaksey's *Daily Telegraph* report began, 'Irish jumping gave its queen a royal welcome home at Navan yesterday when Mrs Charmian Hill's Dawn Run made a majestic start to her new career with a flawless clear round in the Nobber Chase.'

In the *Horse and Hound* he said, 'There had, understandably, been a good deal of heart-searching argument between owner and trainer about the wisdom of starting Dawn Run's new career so early. It is, I think, no secret that Paddy Mullins would have preferred to stick to hurdling for at least one further season.

'But Mrs Charmian Hill is every bit as determined as her great mare and arguing, among other things, that the longer horses go on hurdling, the harder they find it to adapt to fences, she stuck firmly to the decision.'

He concluded, 'So Mrs Hill's beloved champion has reinforced and added to her claim to be the most exciting jumper in training – probably the most exciting female jumper there has ever been.' Truly, it seemed the chasing world lay at her feet.

In early December 1984, Dawn Run strained a ligament under a fore pastern during normal exercise. It did not appear too serious, and thankfully was not the all-important tendon, but she was very sore and it was slow to respond to treatment. She was sound by Christmas, but caution was exercised and she did not run again.

'Who knows, it may be the best thing in the world,' a naturally disappointed Charmian Hill said. 'She is only seven and has been racing hard since she was four. I hope she will come back bigger and stronger than ever.'

All of Ireland, and English National Hunt supporters too, await her reappearance eagerly. Dawn Run and Charmian Hill have stamped an indelible mark on Ireland's rich racing history.

Unique is a dangerous word; but is it likely that ever again a horse of this calibre – champion hurdler of three countries and a mare at that – will be ridden to its first win and exercised regularly by an aged grandmother? That elusive top National Hunt accolade, the Champion Hurdle/Gold Cup double, so far unattained by any horse in history, beckons. The wag in the crowd at Navan called it out for all: 'Now bring us back the Gold Cup!'

Appendix: Dawn Run's Race Record

29.5.82	Clonmel	Corinthian fillies INH Flat Race (Division 2)	Mrs C. D. Hill	8th
17.6.82	Thurles	Devils Bit INH Flat Race	Mrs Hill	4th
22.6.82	Tralee	Castlemaine INH Flat Race	Mrs Hill	won
31.7.82	Galway	Tonroe INH Flat Race	Mr Tom Mullins	won
2.9.82	Tralee	Sean Graham Haversnack Flat Race	Mr Tom Mullins	won
13.11.82	Leopardstown	November Extended Handicap Flat Race	P. V. Gilson	16th
27.11.82	Naas	Kilwarden Maiden Hurdle (Division 2)	P. Kavanagh	4th
20.12.82	Navan	Blackhills Maiden Hurdle	A. Mullins	won
28.12.82	Leopardstown	Findus Beefburger Hurdle	A. Mullins	won
29.1.83	Leopardstown	Delgany Hurdle	A. Mullins	6th
5.2.83	Punchestown	Fournoughts Hurdle	A. Mullins	won
19.2.83	Fairyhouse	Monaloe Extended Handicap Hurdle	A. Mullins	3rd
16.3.83	Cheltenham	Sun Alliance Novices Hurdle	R. Barry	2nd
8.4.83	Liverpool	Page Three Novice Handicap Hurdle	A. Mullins	won
9.4.83	Liverpool	Sun Templegate Hurdle	A. Mullins	2nd
26.4.83	Punchestown	BMW Champion Novices Hurdle	A. Mullins	won
22.10.83	Curragh	Giolla Mear Flat Race	P. V. Gilson	4th
5.11.83	Down Royal	A. R. Soudavar Memorial Trial Hurdle	A. Mullins	won
18.11.83	Ascot	Vat Watkins Hurdle	J. J. O'Neill	won
7.12.83	Naas	Racehorse Trainers Assn Hurdle	J. J. O'Neill	2nd
26.12.83	Kempton	Ladbroke Christmas Hurdle	J. J. O'Neill	won
18.2.84	Leopardstown	Wessel Cable Champion Hurdle	J. J. O'Neill	won
13.3.84	Cheltenham	Waterford Crystal Champion Hurdle	J. J. O'Neill	won

31.3.84	Liverpool	Sandeman Aintree Hurdle	A. Mullins	won
28.5.84	Auteuil	Prix la Barka	A. Mullins	won
22.6.84	Auteuil	Grande Course de Haies D'Auteuil (French Champion Hurdle)	A. Mullins	won
1.11.84	Navan	Nobber Chase	A. Mullins	won